Prais ... ...
Three Bodies
Burning

"What a great read! A work that the reader literally can't put down. It's a rare opportunity for a person on the outside to get a realistic look on the inside of a high level criminal investigation from the perspective of a real professional. Brian Bogdanoff tells the story in a way for all to learn and enjoy."

– Donald Kleine
Head Douglas County Attorney
Omaha, Nebraska

"Bogdanoff's career as a seasoned homicide and drug detective shines through on every page of Three Bodies Burning, as he doggedly pursues justice for three persons murdered and left smoldering in a field outside of Omaha. In this true story, Bogdanoff transfixes the reader as he leads them through the underworld of drugs and violence on his path to solving the crime. "

– Maria Moran
Retired Assistant United States Attorney

"Brian Bogdanoff is one of the best detectives I have worked with in my 27-year career in law enforcement. His extensive experience in narcotics and homicide made him the ideal detective to work the "Three Bodies Burning" case. His ability to tell a story made him the perfect author to share this story. This page turner gives the reader an inside look at how an investigator brought the criminals responsible for this horrific crime to justice."

– Eric Buske
Chief of Police, Bryant, Texas
Retired Chief of Police, Omaha, Nebraska

"An unbelievable book. I've covered court cases and crime, and this is a true crime story you won't want to put down. Bogdanoff includes juice details — and photos — behind a crime that shook up our community. Three Bodies Burning allows readers the unique opportunity to jump inside the mind of an investigator who spent years fighting for justice."

– Shelley Russell
Reporter, FOX 42 News

"Mr. Bogdanoff takes you on a whirlwind tour of a horrific crime, its investigation, its twists and turns, until the conclusion, which results in the prosecution of the perpetrators. This is a fantastic journey into the workings and actions of an outstanding police team of which any city should be proud."

– Robert L. Armstrong and Edwardene Taylor Armstrong
Adjunct Professors, University of Nebraska at Omaha

"Three Bodies Burning is an immensely gripping, fast-paced crime story that reads like the classic thriller. It is exciting, captivating, and almost impossible to put down. This smoothly crafted, at times riveting, narrative is a must read for a first-time author."

– James Martin Davis
Former Special Agent, U.S. Secret Service, One of top 100 trial lawyers in America, a Super Lawyer, and one of Martindale Hubbles Preeminent Lawyers of America

"Three Bodies Burning allures any reader from start to finish in its quest to uncover the truth. It is a fascinating tale involving the perseverance of Bogdanoff along with all the other detectives, crime lab personnel, and DNA analysts to bring the guilty to justice. I thoroughly enjoyed every detail of this true story and found it impossible to put down!"

– Melissa Helligso
Forensic DNA Analyst

"Mr. Bogdanoff spoke at our book club, "The Professional Bookworms." We were so excited to have him come and speak, not only because he is a local author who has gained well-deserved recognition from this book, but he was very open and patient to answering all of our many questions about real-life crime and drama."

– Sharrie Dye
Professional Bookworm Book Club Member

"I purchased this book without any expectations since it was a local crime written by a local Homicide Detective, wow did I get a surprise! The author did a great job writing a superb True Crime book that I have already read twice! I am a faithful Cornwell, Johansen, Rice, Sanford and Patterson reader and this book ranks in my top 2,if not my favorite. I couldn't put it down. There are actual crime scene photos and actual evidence photos included that fed my morbid curiosity. The book was well written! Loved it!!! Would definitely recommend this book."

"The blunt and honest true account that leaves you unable to put it down. I found myself reading all night to know more. This book is destined to be a movie or HBO series one day!"

"Three Bodies Burning is an amazing look at the procedure and process of a complex criminal investigation. More than anything else, the narrative is clear, easy to understand, and allows this tale to unfold from the perspective of a true law enforcement professional and dedicated family man. I don't think that this book would sell as fiction; it is just too fantastic to be anything other than fact. Let's hope that Bogdanoff and his editor revisit this winning formula soon. I'm hooked!"

"...Offers an inside look at the painstakingly long hours detectives must log and the little bits of luck needed to put the bad guys away."

"A fascinating book."

"Bogdanoff has a genuine talent for telling a story; let's hope he treats his readers to many more thrilling tales.

"...it's a pretty good bet few of his neighbors knew of the complicated, often dangerous job Bogdanoff went to every day."

"A handbook for the amateur criminologist, this book is for true crime fans, prosecutors and defense attorneys, and cops and robbers."

"If you like or love details like I do, then dive into this book and enjoy the scary ride that homicide detectives put themselves in every day while they serve our communities."

THREE BODIES BURNING

THE ANATOMY OF AN INVESTIGATION INTO MURDER,
MONEY, AND MEXICAN MARIJUANA

THREE BODIES BURNING

THE ANATOMY OF AN INVESTIGATION INTO MURDER, MONEY, AND MEXICAN MARIJUANA

Brian Bogdanoff

Award-Winning Homicide Detective

Omaha, Nebraska

ISBN13: 978-0-9831298-1-3
Library of Congress Control Number: 2010917273

1161 Press, LLC
P.O. Box 71
Blair, NE 68008
www.ThreeBodiesBurning.com

Crime scene photos used with written permission from the Omaha Chief of Police.

Photo on p. 9 reprinted with permission from *The Omaha World-Herald*.

Warning: This book contains graphic crime scene photos and adult language.

Printed in the United States
10 9 8 7 6 5 4 3

This book is dedicated to children of cops who in a sense are also victims because they lose quality time with parents who are out investigating crime; to spouses who lose the companionship with a life partner who is involved in the investigative process; and to mothers and fathers of cops who never stop worrying about their child's calling and the fact that they are always battling the evil element.

THE HOMICIDE INVESTIGATOR

No greater honor will ever be bestowed on an officer or a more profound duty imposed on him or her than when he or she is entrusted with the investigation of the death of a human being.

It is his or her duty to find the facts, regardless of color or creed, without prejudice, and to let no power on earth deter him or her from presenting these facts to the court without regard to personality.

—Anonymous

CONTENTS

AUTHOR'S NOTE

Bringing the bad guys to justice takes hard work, patience, and luck. It's about following the leads, making your own leads, and hoping for that lucky break that's less about luck and more about being at the right place at the right time—and having the street smarts to know a break when it bites you in the ass.

I spent a majority of my career working in narcotics, gang, and homicide units. During that time, I wrote tens of thousands of police reports, search warrants, and even wiretaps. I made drug buys, chased down suspects, arrested plenty of dealers, and took them off the streets.

Writing this book is the culmination of a law enforcement career that spanned over twenty years. And this case has it all: drugs, guns, murder, and sound detective and forensic work that put bad guys behind bars for life. That's the stuff of police work, and it's not always like you see on TV cop shows. Yes, I got that lucky break too.

All the material in this book is derived from my own personal observation as a homicide detective in the pursuit of justice in this case and from official police records and interviews.

Names have been changed to protect the true identities of cooperating characters because they have gone on with their lives. I've even changed my own name. In this story, I am Bo Harrison. The real story lies in the behind-the-scenes police work most people never see (not even on TV). This is the story of a drug deal gone bad.

Over most of my career, I have volunteered time as a speaker in local high schools regarding search and seizure and general policing. During these talks, I would bring hundreds of real life pictures, showing drugs, guns, and bad guys. I would play actual audiotapes of myself making undercover drug purchases, with these suspects being arrested.

These props generated hours filled with questions, and I would generally give an answer with a story from my career. At the end of one class, a student said to me that I should write a book with these stories. That was the beginning of this project. I know I was a good cop. I now hope I am an entertaining author and you enjoy the book.

1
MURDER
IN THE HEARTLAND

A beautiful spring day. The mercury in the thermometer showed temps up into the 50s and 60s, which was so greatly needed in the Midwest after the bitter cold of winter. Small leaves were starting to break open from buds on the trees and shrubs. The good feeling of spring life was in the air.

In just a few weeks, college baseball would have its spotlight right here in Omaha, Nebraska, the home of the College World Series. Nebraska . . . "The Good Life" is the state's motto implying, I guess, a better way of life here in the heartland.

A Tuesday morning in early May 2005 started normally in this city with a metro population of nearly a million. Workers begin to commute into the city from suburbs and towns in all directions.

During the six o'clock hour, with dawn breaking over the eastern Iowa hills, one commuter coming from the northern outskirts of the city sees what he thinks is a small brush fire in an overgrown, wooded area, off to the side of the road.

This brushy area has the feel of country and serenity dense with foliage and trees. Several neighborhoods are nestled into this scenic and peaceful area—country living on the edge of the metropolitan area.

The commuter uses his cell phone to call 911 to report the brush fire. As the 911 operators broadcast this brush fire over the radio waves to the fire department, it is also simulcast on the police radio frequencies. An alert uniform patrol officer in the area responds to this radio transmission of the brush fire to aid the fire department with any traffic control, if needed.

The officer arrives before the fire department and does in fact locate a fire about fifty feet off the side of the road, in a heavily wooded area, which in dawning daylight now was protected from visibility from the street. But at night in the darkness the site would have been almost undetectable.

The officer pulls his cruiser off the road and gets out to observe the fire, which is exactly what any cop would do in an effort to get the best vantage point to watch the fire department do their thing. It is human nature. Everybody loves to watch the firefighters put out the fire. It's also true that everybody loves the firemen—the heroes who put out fires and save cats from trees—and nobody likes the cops who are always pissing somebody off with a speeding or parking ticket.

As the officer is claiming his front-row seat, he can't believe his eyes. He broadcasts to the 911 operators, "Be advised. I'm at the brush fire, but it appears to be three bodies burning."

This is obviously more complex than the original brush fire call. Things now must be considered, such as securing the crime scene, which is currently on fire, and putting out the fire in a manner that destroys the least amount of possible evidence.

The officer made a smart decision fairly quickly: to put out the fire with his hand-held extinguisher from the trunk of his cruiser. This is actually surprising because, in general, during my twenty years as an officer on the Omaha police force, if something could get screwed up, it usually did. This is not to lay any blame on anybody, but very few times do the good guys, the cops, catch a break or get lucky.

This quick decision by the young, first-responding officer enabled many things to take place that were essential for a successful crime scene investigation. Most important, it enabled additional patrol cars to come quickly and set up perimeters with both an inner and an outer crime scene so it would not be compromised by a bunch of law enforcement personnel inadvertently walking through the crime scene or over-eager media people trampling on vital evidence.

Once those three words "three bodies burning" went out over the radio, every cop, firefighter, and media person is going to try to get as close as they can to get a peek, whether by walking, driving, or somehow sneaking in to say they were there. On this day, that did not happen. Life is good.

The homicide detectives now have to try to figure out what happened. Who are these victims? And who did this to them?

It was a good day for the good guys. An alert citizen reported a problem and a smart cop discovered a crime scene and protected the evidence with quick action in putting out the fire. It was a bad day for the three dead people who were set on fire.

2
CRIME SCENE: JOURNEY FOR THE TRUTH

The crime scene is a crucial part of every homicide investigation. It is at this point that the journey begins in an attempt to find the truth about what happened.

Documentation of the crime scene is the responsibility of the homicide detective who is assigned the case. During the crime scene investigation, the scene is documented by photography, by written report, and by the collection of evidence with the assistance of the crime lab technicians, and, in this case, arson investigators because of the fire aspect.

This crime scene was unique. First, the condition and position of the bodies was bizarre. The bodies were still smoking, lying nearly naked in a wooded area. Black burn marks were evident where some of the accelerant touched the bodies. Second, the overall size of the scene was larger than most.

The first homicide detectives on the scene soon noticed that blood trails on the road adjacent to where the bodies were found in both north and south directions, for approximately a fourth to a half mile in each direction. The crime scene was divided into two quadrants. The inner crime scene was the area where the bodies were located, and the outer crime scene contained the blood trails on the road in both directions. The inner crime scene consisted of the three bodies lying like cordwood. The clothing on the bodies appeared to be in disarray as if the pants had been pulled down near mid-thigh, exposing some genitalia.

Good investigators quickly have thoughts running through their minds. *Was this an unusual type of staging by the suspects? Was this a sign of disrespect? The call signature of a specific gang? Is there some connection to a sexual act?* No one knows, but these are just thoughts that start to fire in a detective's mind at the onset of a case. Having these thoughts is normal and good in the investigative process. But the investigator must not come to any conclusions based on these observations. The investigative process will answer these questions.

Omaha police officers guard the outer perimeter of the crime scene as detectives trace the blood trail on the street. Reprinted with permission from *The Omaha World-Herald*.

The victims all appeared to be Hispanic because of their darker skin and black hair. One victim was very large in stature, six feet tall, 300 pounds, in his mid-twenties, with clean-cut black hair.

The dump site: Three burning bodies were found stacked like cordwood in a wooded area. Note the leg on the closest victim is completely burned away. Clothing has burned away and pants were found down near their ankles or lower legs.

Close-up of blood trail found on the street leading to the dump site.

The second victim was slender, also six feet tall, 180 pounds, clean-cut hair, also in his twenties, with a large dark-blue, five-pointed star tattoo on his abdomen.

The third burned victim was a Hispanic male with a stocky build, five feet eight or so, 250 pounds, in his late thirties. He was wearing cowboy boots, jeans, and a Western-style plaid shirt. This type of clothing is common with men who have an association to Mexico.

All three victims appeared to have trauma to their skulls that would be consistent with gunshot wounds (in other words, not cop talk, we saw gunshot wounds to their heads); however, this would not be confirmed until later at the autopsies. In addition, all victims had burns on different portions of their bodies where it had appeared that an accelerant had been applied to the bodies, causing the burning to occur in a pattern where the accelerant was touching the body.

The inner crime scene also revealed multiple vehicle tire tracks coming into it from the road several car lengths, then stopping, with the closest track still being about twenty-five feet from the bodies. These tracks would end up leading nowhere in the investigation because this area was a popular location with locals for the springtime sport of mushroom hunting, in which people walk through the woods looking for morel mushrooms, which are considered a delicacy by some.

The wooded area was just off to the east on a fairly well traveled rural two-lane paved road that dipped and climbed like a roller coaster. The site where the bodies were dumped was at one of the dips in the road, off to the side, well away from any of the homes set back in the wooded terrain and just north of the outskirts of the elite Omaha Country Club golf course.

Due to the multiple overlapping sets of tracks and the moist soil conditions, no distinctive track could be identified or associated with the three burning bodies.

The outer crime scene produced interesting blood tracks. These blood tracks appeared to be in a symmetrical pattern. Blood seemed to fall to the paved road in lines that were approximately five to six inches across from each other, but the distance between the drops in each line varied. It appeared that the distances between drops were larger the farther away from the area where the bodies were.

We analyzed these track patterns. We thought the lines resulted from what we speculated as pooling blood running out the grooves in the bed of a truck and, depending on the speed of the truck, the distance between the drops or puddles varied.

Markers were set up to show the pattern of these blood trails in a dimension so the path could be followed more easily. The pattern of these blood trails showed that the truck drove past the dump site where the bodies were located and pulled into two different gravel inlets, then backed up, turned around, and pulled into a third inlet where the bodies were found. The amount of blood that was either located in one specific area or had distances between the blood droplets depended on the speed of the truck.

This was all theory, of course, at this point and, ultimately, a witness or co-conspirator would have to confirm this theory. Nonetheless, these were physical pieces of evidence that could corroborate a statement by a witness or co-conspirator if one was ever located. The documentation of this crime scene took over sixteen hours, and during these sixteen hours, luck was very much on law enforcement's side because the weather had held.

At any given time in the Midwest, during the spring, a thunderstorm or tornado or just a simple rain shower could appear in the calmest of days. If that happened, evidence could be lost. But it did not happen on this day.

3
NOTHING ARTISTIC
IN THIS CANVASS

"Bo, we got three dead guys dumped and set on fire. I need you to get to the outer perimeter and a briefing will take place there," said my Sergeant, Harry Bogowski, in an early morning phone call. This is where my part in this journey begins. My name is Bo Harrison. I am an Omaha police officer working as a homicide detective.

When these calls come in, I usually scramble for a piece of paper and pen to write down all the information, but this one was simple. I was already dressed for work and said hello and goodbye to my wife and kids on my way out the door. As I was driving to the briefing location, I wondered how screwed up this case would be based on the sergeant's phone call.

After arriving at the outer perimeter, I met with Sgt. Bogowski and most of the day-shift homicide unit. The first piece of good news was that Detective Isadore Demann had gotten the crime scene assignment. This was good news for a couple of reasons. First, Isadore Demann is a superb investigator, and this crime scene was not going to be simple in any way to document, but I knew he would do a good job. He's squared away, thorough in his documentation, relentless and would leave no stone unturned. In police circles, he was a real swinging dick.

Second, not that I was being lazy, but I had just finished a double murder jury trial on an international narcotics drug conspiracy murder between Arizona and Nebraska that took a year to investigate, and these three burned bodies did not feel like a ground ball investigation. (A ground ball investigation is a very simple one.) As a general rule, the officer assigned as crime scene investigator was usually assigned the case, so I was thinking, "Congratulations to Isadore Demann on now being the new owner of this case."

The canvassing of a crime scene area is a basic investigative tool. Canvassing consists of making contact with residents or businesses in the general area of the crime scene. During this contact, the investigators identify themselves to the residents or business owners, inform them of the investigation, and, during this interaction, take down any information that could be of significance.

This legwork is important because often people will not initiate a contact to the police on their own. Direct contact opens up an avenue of communication. If there is no one to talk to at a business or a residence, we leave a business card so that follow-up can take place.

Knock, knock. I couldn't find a doorbell at this house near the crime scene in a neighborhood of acreages and nice homes a half mile away. I was going door to door. Many people were already gone—to work. Others were just getting up.

"Yes?" asked a thirty-something young woman who carefully opened the door and saw me standing on her front porch.

"Hi, I'm Officer Harrison of the Omaha police," I said. I held up my badge. "I don't know if you know. Some bodies were found not far from here. Did you hear any noises or any vehicles? Anything out of the ordinary that you would consider suspicious?"

This pattern went on for sixteen hours. After walking miles, knocking on hundreds of doors, and talking to dozens of people at their houses or businesses and dropping off dozens of business cards, all members of the homicide unit met back at central police headquarters to debrief what had been learned. The canvass produced nothing.

The crime scene was described by Sgt. Bogowski and Detective Demann. During their description of the crime scene, we learned additional pieces of information.

"The bodies were cleaned before they were dumped," Sgt. Bogowski told us. "There was no personal property on them. No wallets. No watches. No jewelry. No nothing. Except a hotel receipt on one of them, and a piece of paper inside another stiff's pocket."

One of these pieces of paper was described as a hotel receipt to a hotel in the southwest area of Omaha, which was going to be followed up immediately after this briefing. This hotel receipt was found on the youngest Hispanic male who had the star tattoo on his abdomen. The receipt bore the name of Barry Willis.

The second piece of evidence was a small, torn piece of paper that was approximately six inches by four inches with six columns of numbers and each column totaled. There were 140 numbers in these columns that ranged from 26.2 to 14, but the general numbers ranged between 20 and 22. The total number of all these columns was 2,920.4.

"Bo, does this look like some sort of drug record?" Sgt. Bogowski asked me.

I wasn't sure. If you looked at the total number of 2,920.4, and if it represented ounces and/or grams, it did not seem consistent with the way cocaine or methamphetamine would be packaged. This was based on an ounce weighing 28 grams, but none of these numbers were actually 28 grams, all were much smaller and, based on my experience in the narcotics unit, if someone was dealing at a high level and was selling ounce quantities, the ounce quantities would be exact.

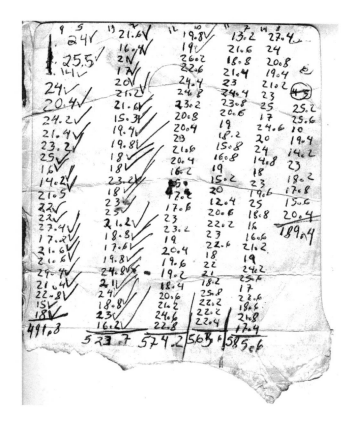

The list of numbers found in the pocket of the victim who became known as John Doe 3.

If, in fact, someone was selling this many ounces, they wouldn't calculate it in ounce quantities, they would calculate it in pounds or even kilograms. If these numbers meant either kilograms or pounds of cocaine or methamphetamine, these numbers would be extremely high for any investigation in Omaha.

I personally had never heard of 2,900 pounds of cocaine being in the metro area. Even if I thought this was referring to marijuana, this quantity was also extremely large for anything known from past investigations.

"Right now, it doesn't look like a drug record," I told him. Boy, was I going to be wrong.

Autopsies were scheduled to be performed the following morning and the follow-up at the southwest area hotel would take place right after the briefing.

4
THE BODIES
TELL A STORY

An autopsy is the post-death examination of a body by a pathologist. At this examination an attempt is made to determine the cause of death. Evidence is collected from the body, which includes the clothing and samples of fluids, hair, tissue, urine, and blood. The victim's clothes are searched again and taken into evidence.

The crime scene investigator attends the autopsy and provides any background or insight that the pathologist may need regarding the crime scene that could be significant at the autopsy. Also present is a member of the crime lab, who actually takes photographs of the entire procedure, and an assistant to the pathologist, who is a full-time employee at the morgue, and who helps prepare the body. It is often a two-person job to maneuver these bodies, as they have become stiff and are literally "dead weight" to move around.

The assistant who works at the morgue has worked there for many years and is also a superb chef who specializes in cheesecake. It is not uncommon to attend an autopsy at the county morgue and be offered a slice of cheesecake.

In the metropolitan area, the coroner is actually an attorney with the County Attorney's office. The coroner is not to be confused with the pathologist, who is the actual medical doctor who performs the autopsy examination, pronouncing the cause of death. The coroner signs the death certificate. In the Omaha area, a group of pathologists rotate duty days so one pathologist does not perform all autopsies. I had heard once that the going rate the pathologist receives for an autopsy is $1,800 per autopsy, so multiply that times the number of bodies, which was three, and this case was not a bad haul for the doctor.

Some cops really get into the autopsy investigation. They enjoy getting right next to the corpse and watching every cut the pathologist makes. Myself, I am not that excited about autopsies in general. During my recruit training, nearly twenty years earlier, I had a bad experience at an autopsy that we were ordered to attend as part of the training curriculum. When conducting an inspection of the brain, the doctor carefully cuts out the top of the skull using a small electric zip saw. During this cutting process, a chip of the dead person's skull flew at me and landed right on my lower lip.

I didn't puke then, but I have to admit that I have vomited on more than one occasion around dead bodies. It was usually the stinkers that got to me. A stinker is a body that has not been found for several days. During the decomposing process, the body can really start smelling foul. To this day, if I just think about that dead smell, I retch.

Imagine a natural death, for example. Let's say nobody has heard from grandpa for a few days. So a family member calls the cops. Patrol officers go to grandpa's door, but they don't even have to go in. They can smell the dead smell. And that's when they call in the homicide detectives. We show up and get in the door. There's grandpa, looking like a shriveled up raisin in white briefs as his body fluids expand and darken the skin. He's most likely found in bed as death came silently and quickly in the night.

A natural death, we think, and most probably the coroner will confirm it, but the smell sticks with you. Once we move the body to look for clues, we break the skin membrane, and that smell bursts out even stronger. At those times, I've been known to run into the yard or find a corner to puke in.

In general, I was a homicide investigator with a fairly weak stomach. Knowing that, when I would go to an autopsy, I generally stood as far away from the examination table as possible, and when the pathologist said that he had found something of interest, I would step up, observe the item of significance, and then step to the back row, which was fine with me.

Specifically, during this autopsy, the victims were labeled as John Doe 1, John Doe 2, and John Doe 3 because they had not been positively identified at the time the autopsies began.

John Doe 1 was the twenty-year-old, six-foot Hispanic who weighed about 300 pounds. He had a gunshot wound to the right side of the skull and bullet fragments located inside his brain. Burn marks were located on several portions of his body in a pattern that would be consistent with someone splashing accelerant such as gasoline on him. Where it had touched his body, it burned through his lower legs. His feet and ankles were burned completely away from his body. No identification or jewelry was located on him. He had been wearing a T-shirt and jeans. The jeans were just as we found him in the burning field—pulled down near mid-thigh to knee area, exposing the genitals.

During the inspection of the body, we saw no signs of sexual conduct or assault: no semen was found, no penetration in any orifices. Probably no sexual assault, even though the scene looked suspiciously sexual because the bodies were nearly naked.

How could that be? We speculated that their shirts had burned away. Their pants were down around their legs because, imagine this: you're the bad guys pulling dead bodies out of a truck. These victims were large men. Even with two people lifting and tugging, hauling them from the shooting scene, into and out of a truck, would be tough. And if the shooters grabbed the victims' clothing, the loosely worn pants would naturally pull down.

During the shaving of the hair on the head of this victim, stippling was observed around the wound. Stippling is small markings around an entrance wound caused by the burning gunpowder that travels only inches, which would indicate that the weapon was fired up close to the victim's head.

No question. The cause of death was the gunshot wound to the head. It was also determined during the autopsy that the death occurred before the fire, because there were no signs of inhalation of soot or smoke in the lungs, mouth, throat, or nostrils of the victim. In other words, he was dead before the fire started. Otherwise, we would have seen the smoke in his lungs if he had been breathing.

John Doe 2 was also Hispanic, also in his twenties, six feet tall and not as heavy as the first victim. He weighed about 180 pounds. We saw a gunshot wound to the left side of the skull and also a corresponding "through and through" wound to his left hand in what appeared to be a defense wound. During the autopsy, this was confirmed when the hand was raised and a rod was slid through the hand wound leading directly to the head wound. Bullet fragments were located inside the brain.

This victim also had a gunshot wound to the left upper shoulder and a third gunshot wound near the back shoulder. Bullet fragments were located in the torso from these bullet wounds. Stippling was observed on the hand wound, but not on the head wound. Burned portions on this body were also at random, where an apparent accelerant had been splashed. His clothing also consisted of blue jeans and a T-shirt, with the pants around the mid-thigh area, but again no signs of any type of sexual assault.

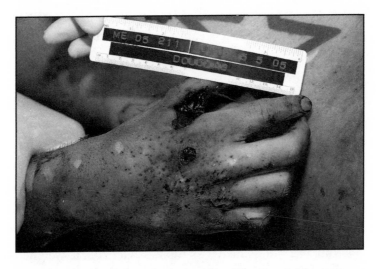

Stippling on a hand wound was noted on John Doe 2. The entrance and exit wound indicates he likely raised his hand in defense with the bullet passing through his hand and entering his head. This victim's star tattoo on his torso is noted.

More gunshot wounds with John Doe 3, a Hispanic guy in his mid-thirties. He was five feet eight and 250 pounds. A gunshot entrance wound was seen to the top of the head with stippling from the close-up shot. Bullet fragments were located inside the brain. This was the victim who wore Western-style cowboy clothing. His teeth were in very poor condition, which would indicate that he had very little or no dental care during his lifetime. His pants were also pulled down to his ankles; however, no signs of a sexual assault were apparent.

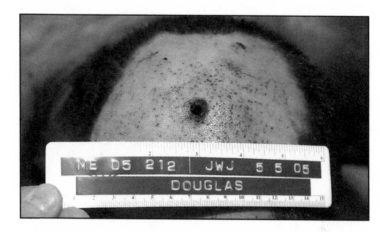

The victim's hair has been shaved to reveal the fatal gunshot wound and stippling to the top of the head.

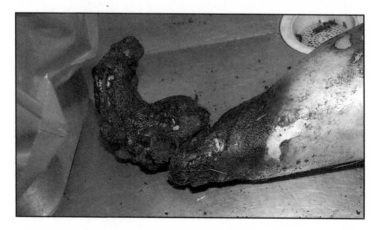

The lower calf, ankle area, and foot of John Doe 1. This shows the intensity of the fire where the accelerant was used.

Overall, the three autopsies took nine hours to complete. During the process, the pathologist and arson investigator were measuring the depth of the burns on the bodies to determine how long the bodies had been burning before the fire was put out. That would help establish a time frame from when the bodies were dumped and burned until they were discovered.

Three victims. Who were they? Gunshots fired close up. Who fired the gun? Where were they killed? Now we had to figure out the rest of the story.

5
WHO ARE YOU?

By the time the second day of this investigation was under way, the news media were in full gear. Reporters were actually caught attempting to get into the inner crime scene on the first day by going cross-country through the woods. These news parasites were trying to get a picture for the next day's paper or newscast.

I'm sure they think some amendment gives them that right, but screw that right. If they contaminate some piece of evidence or publish a graphic photo of the bodies that could negate a statement obtained later with information known only to someone with first-hand knowledge of the crime scene, it could hurt the case.

In general, the media are a pain in the butt, only looking to sensationalize a situation to promote their own product. However, that said, they can also be used as a tool during some investigations.

In addition to the news media frenzy, we followed up on the hotel receipt, which led us to a residence in Phoenix, Arizona. We were able to determine fairly quickly who John Doe 1 and John Doe 2 were. Family members of both men confirmed that they were in the Omaha, Nebraska, area and provided photographs of them to law enforcement to compare to the bodies. In addition, fingerprints were obtained from databases in Arizona, which also positively confirmed their identities.

These two victims were identified as Ricardo Gomez, who went by the nickname "Richie" and his half-brother, Barry Willis. John Doe 3 was later identified as Floreno Gonzalez; however, his positive identification was eventually made by a DNA comparison with DNA extracted from a family member. Positive identification could not be made with his face or hands because they were too badly burned. These initial phone conversations and contacts with family members did not provide a great amount of detail as to why these guys were in Omaha or what the relationship was between the two half-brothers and Floreno Gonzalez.

Now, the investigative process—the journey—could continue. We needed to find as much information about our victims as we could so we could catch their killers.

6
THE FANCY
BLACK TRUCK

By now, day two, the calls were pouring in. Business cards that had been left at houses and businesses during the canvass were being found by people who were now returning calls to the homicide unit. These calls, even if no information was gained, were valuable because people could then be eliminated from a lead sheet as a possible source of information, closing that lead for the investigators.

During these first few days, an interesting call came in as a result of the canvass. A man who lived near the area of the outer crime scene where the bodies were located told me he drives to work every morning at about 5:30 and crosses the intersection of Sixtieth and State that was to the south of the crime scene. The caller explained generally at that time of morning in this fairly secluded area, there is never any vehicle traffic. But on the morning the bodies were discovered, he approached the intersection and was stopped at the stop sign, facing toward another vehicle.

The caller described this vehicle as a black truck that he thought was newer and had a fancy style to it, similar to a Chevy Avalanche. The caller stated not only was it unusual to be face to face with a vehicle at the intersection during this time of the morning, but this contact was strange in another way. It was as if both stopped parties were at a stalemate, each waiting for an abnormally long time for the other one to go through the intersection first.

The truck during this "standoff," the caller said, had a turn signal flashing. The caller said he went ahead and proceeded through the intersection, but looked in his rearview mirror and observed the truck continue straight and not turn as the turn signal had indicated. I documented the details from this call in a supplemental report. The details from this call would later resurface as the case unfolded and the facts developed.

Another significant development occurred during the first few days. A car rented by Barry Willis was located abandoned on the shoulder of Highway 75 at least twenty-five miles south of the metropolitan area—and about twenty-eight miles from where the bodies were discovered. This vehicle was a dark green Pontiac G6.

Inspection of the car showed no visible signs of foul play. It was just left on the side of the road: no property in it, no keys, no anything.

A complete forensic search was conducted on this vehicle, which consisted of vacuuming the interior, swabbing all handles and knobs or any area that would likely have physical contact with a person and reveal fingerprints, as well as photographing the vehicle. These items of possible evidence would be maintained in the police property room for future reference if suspects were ever developed and DNA comparisons could be made of the swabs taken.

7
WHO AM I?

At the time this investigation began, I was an eighteen-year veteran of the Omaha Police Department, a lifelong resident of the area, and someone whose life path probably prepared me well for police work and dealing with people of all backgrounds.

In 1978, I was part of the second year of mandatory busing in the public school system. *Desegregation* was the term used for this busing process. As a result, as a white kid from West Omaha, I spent about two hours a day on a school bus. The school I attended was right in the middle of the North Omaha neighborhoods known as the "hood."

I participated in most school activities, played on most of the sports teams, and developed interpersonal skills with kids from all races and backgrounds. I remember that the race part of the whole situation meant more to the adults than it did to us kids. To this day, I can name several of my friends from that time period that I would never have met had it not been for busing.

From this school, I went to an inner-city high school that had a great mixture of all cultures and socioeconomic levels. At Central High School, some of the most gifted minds and some of the real dough heads in the city all attended. I probably was about in the middle of this group. It was at this high school that I saw my first stabbing victim. I will never forget watching this kid with his hands on his stomach and his intestines squishing through his fingers as he was walking to the nurse's office.

It was also during these years and going back even further when I was twelve and worked for my father in his plastering and drywall business that I developed my work ethic. To this day I still believe that no matter how hard I worked in the law enforcement field, it is nothing compared to the long hours and hard labor my father put in every day in his business.

As a result of working at this drywall and plastering company, I generally was helping one of the laborers, hauling or toting material to some job site. To describe these laborers, it would be nice to say that they were a little rough around the edges, but they were actually very interesting and fun guys to be around. It was during these contacts and relations that I learned stuff about life that no school could provide. Later, I would encounter many of these guys and some of their relatives in my life as a police officer. Unfortunately, we were on opposite sides of the law.

After high school, I enrolled at the University of Nebraska at Omaha and after about two years of an undecided major, I took a class called Deviant Behaviors in the Criminal Justice Department. I liked it and took more criminal justice classes, eventually getting an internship with the Omaha Police Department in 1985.

My assignment in this internship was the youth services unit. The detectives were assigned runaways and missing person cases, which were put in a big book as active missing cases. I started reading the case files and making follow-up calls and located many of the missing kids on my own. The case officers loved it because I was doing their work.

Then, in 1986, a boy was abducted and the case was assigned to the unit. Two weeks later, the boy was found dead on the outskirts of the city. A task force was quickly organized to investigate this crime, and I became a call taker on a hotline for this investigation. My fate was sealed from that point on. I wanted to be a cop.

By 1988, I was hired and attended the training academy of the Omaha Police Department. Not long before this, street gang activity had begun in the Omaha area, and crack cocaine was causing havoc in the lower socioeconomic areas. Also during this time, volumes of negative press coverage stemmed around the violence and drug dealing in the Northeast quadrant of the community, specifically revolving around government housing projects.

The mayor and police chief announced the implementation of foot patrols (called Beat Patrols) in the housing projects. Because I was one of the lowest three officers in seniority, my first job was to walk a foot patrol in a housing project in the north metropolitan area—for the next two years.

My first two partners were academy classmates of mine. Both came from small-town rural backgrounds. We worked four days on and two days off, alternating, so you worked two days with one partner, then two days with the second partner, then the next two days were your days off.

What an environment—walking on foot all night, from six in the evening until two in the morning, in the largest housing project in the Omaha area called "Little Vietnam" because of all the violence. We quickly became familiar with crack cocaine and violence. We witnessed cars from rival gangs driving through the projects, sticking guns out of the windows and doing drive-by shootings.

We heard gunshots every day. I remember once talking to an eighteen-year-old girl who was walking with her three-year-old child in the projects. After speaking for a short time and walking around a project building, we heard gunshots. Upon running back to the sound of the shots, my partner and I saw this young mother on the ground with a small-caliber gunshot wound right between her eyes. She died right there on the spot. That homicide is still unsolved to this day.

On beat patrol in the Logan-Fontenelle projects
(Little Vietnam), about 1991.

Despite these tragedies, it was actually a fulfilling job. I believe that we did make life more comfortable for people who were not involved in the thug gang member lifestyle.

One area in the projects was referred to as the horseshoe. It was basically a U-shaped drive off one of the perimeter main streets. This drive created a convenient location for thugs to congregate and sell drugs. In an attempt to combat this activity, we would go into an old, condemned building adjacent to the horseshoe and climb up to the roof of the building, gaining a surveillance point for this area. This vantage point created probable cause because we could observe the criminal acts, such as selling crack cocaine.

Routinely, the sellers would hide the drugs on the ground or in drain pipes or somewhere creative. We would then watch a few deals go down, learn the routine, and then call in a cruiser to secure the dealers and recover the evidence. Even more beautiful was the knowledge we gained by watching these guys and how they interacted. We were often so close we could hear their conversations, learning their jargon and slang.

My career was filled with many crazy experiences. One night we were out of the projects because a large crowd had gathered around a bar several blocks to the north. The Beat Patrol officers decided to do some surveillance on the rear alley of this bar because guys were obviously walking back to this area, and we believed drugs might be stashed in the dark shadows of this alley.

After about thirty minutes of surveillance through binoculars, I saw a guy stuff a white package about four inches by eight inches down the front of his pants. At this point in my career, I had never seen a kilo or any large quantity of cocaine in real life, but that was what I surely believed was being hidden down the front of this guy's pants.

I told the other two officers about what I had just seen, so we decided to check this guy out. We approached in the shadows of the alley on foot, and just as we got within eight feet, I stepped on a fallen tree branch. It snapped. The guy who stuffed the white object down his pants turned toward me and pulled the white thing out of the waist of his pants. A sawed-off shotgun. The white that I saw was tape he had put on the butt of the gun where he had cut it down.

As he turned, I didn't even have my gun out. He leveled the shotgun right on me. Click. It misfired. He dropped the gun and started to run, but was tackled within a heartbeat. Holy shit! The gun was recovered, loaded. It just didn't fire. One of the lucky breaks of my career.

The guy told us he was going into the bar to rob it because he had been down on his luck. He apologized, stating he was just reacting when he turned and pointed the gun at me, not knowing that I was a police officer.

Another memorable moment in my career was during a festival called Native Omaha Days, which has a parade, dances, and several events celebrating the city's African-American community. During the day and evening hours, everything is generally positive, but every year, after the sun goes down, things get wild, with gunshots fired and police usually having to clear the entire area, shutting down the festival.

One year, the officers from the Beat Patrol were on foot patrolling the area during the daylight hours, just walking around the crowd and talking to people. Everything was cool. All of a sudden, we encountered a drunk guy who was causing problems at one of the booths that was set up just to the east of the main festival area. We tried to walk him out of the area, keeping the peace and not causing a problem for anyone involved. But this gentleman started yelling, and a crowd started to form.

This situation is so typical when dealing with drunk people. He could not comprehend that we were not looking to arrest him. We were just trying to stop him from bothering other people. Eventually it escalated to a point where he attempted to push me, which is not cool, but still, our ultimate objective was to remove this guy from the area.

Then, this drunk guy takes a half-assed swing at me. This cannot be tolerated and can actually incite things to get even more out of control. So, without hesitation, I decide he must be stopped quickly. I employed a simple leg sweep, which is kicking the target's legs out from underneath him. The idea is to get the person to the ground quickly, cuff him, and get him out of the crowd.

It sounded like a nice plan, except my leg sweep didn't go as planned. As I struck his leg, the leg flew off the drunk guy's body, through the air, and landed fifteen feet away. I had no idea it was a fake leg. The crowd went quiet. You could hear a pin drop. It was a sight that the mind could not process. I ran over and grabbed the leg like I was an all-star wrestler and the crowd cheered. Go figure. That could have gone either way. It could have been a riot, but the crowd was actually happy with our actions. We gave this guy his leg back, escorted him a few blocks away, and let him go.

Another set of lessons I learned during these early years occurred while conducting what we called a bar check. A bar check was a simple act where we were instructed to walk into bars in plain view, in uniform, make contact with the people inside, say hello, and while doing this, it was routine that either guns or drugs would be found on the floor. This practice really did not produce many arrests, but it sure recovered numerous drugs and guns, and that was a good thing considering how each of these items had such a negative impact on society.

One night, there was a large volume of foot and vehicle traffic in the parking lot of a bar that was directly next to one of the housing projects. So, as normal, we made contact with our immediate command and indicated we would be conducting a bar check at this location. We went inside, made contact with the people, and left after only a few minutes. It was obvious while inside the bar that this was a crowd not likely to ditch drugs or guns on the floor. This crowd was well dressed and very professional looking, so we left rather quickly.

While I was inside, I actually had a cordial, but quick, conversation with one woman, asking her about the evening and how the food was. We left the bar and reported the contact to our immediate command, who was outside in the parking lot. It appeared this was a very routine, non-problematic situation.

The next day, the news media were reporting a harassing attack on leaders of the African-American community. These political and civic leaders claimed they were threatened, harassed, and intimidated by officers coming into a celebration they were having. When I first heard these news accounts, I was trying to figure out what bar it was and who these officers were. I then learned it was our bar check from the previous night.

After a few weeks of continuous negative news, the chief of police at the time bowed to political pressure and suspended the four officers (including me) for eight days and gave reprimands to the sergeant and lieutenant who were on duty at the time. In the end, we fought our suspensions and had a full-blown personnel hearing regarding the situation. After all the witnesses were called, our suspensions were overturned with the board issuing a statement that people's perceptions of the incidents can vary, but the actions we conducted were not wrong.

I guess that was a nice way of preventing any embarrassment to the leaders of that community who made the accusations. Lucky for me that chief of police did not last much longer, so my career path progressed without any retribution. I learned several lessons from that incident, such as the value of my immediate command having qualities like loyalty and a true understanding of right and wrong.

I also learned that I would face people in this job who have certain agendas, and to support those agendas, they will manipulate situations and facts. In dealing with these types of people, my first course of action would be to stay as far away from them as possible. But if during an investigation, these lines would be crossed again, it was always my policy to have as much evidence as possible supporting my law enforcement actions, so they could not have a voice.

I was then recruited to the narcotics unit by the beginning of my fourth year on the job. I was assigned to a night shift crew that developed outstanding narcotics investigations and arrest statistics that, I've been told, dominated every other crew in the history of the Omaha Police Department.

The basic narcotics investigation formula was rather simple and had to follow a set pattern using one or more of a few tactics to achieve the goal. For instance, the development and cultivation of informants was the main source that either made you a productive narcotics officer or not. To produce an informant, you have to have interpersonal and communication skills. If you don't have those, nobody from the street will work with you. Believe me, I know narcotics guys who worked for years in the narcotics unit and never did develop their own informants.

The next question is, "Where do these informants come from?" They can come from anywhere. A call could come into the narcotics unit secretary from a citizen, who eventually becomes an informant. Everyone you arrest should be evaluated to determine if they could be a good informant, and, usually, if a person was arrested, the motivation to cooperate is certainly there if it could lessen their charges.

Once you have informants, they can assist in different types of investigations, such as developing probable cause on search warrants by simply seeing drugs in a house, or they can wear a wire and make purchases of narcotics on audiotape and testify in court to the incident. Informants can introduce undercover officers to drug dealers, and then the officers actually buy the drugs, leaving the informant out of future deals.

Every so often, a wiretap investigation develops, often with the aid of informants leading officers to the targets and their specific telephone numbers. The probable cause is developed further by listening to the phone calls regarding the drug dealings, along with surveillance on the bad guy, ultimately leading to the arrest of not just the main target of the wiretap, but all the people above and below the target in the entire conspiracy of drug dealing.

Another tactic that we used in narcotics investigations is called the "knock and talk." This is done when probable cause is not yet developed either because it could not be developed after trying or because of time constraints, such as other investigations or the information was beginning to become stale. When this happened, we would do a "knock and talk," which is the simple process of approaching the suspected individual's house and knocking on the door.

"I'm Officer Harrison with Omaha police," I would say at the door, big smile on my face. "We received a complaint that there might be some narcotics activity here. I'm not saying there is or there isn't, but I want to clear the complaint. To do that, if you grant me permission to search and we find no drugs, then I'll close out this complaint."

I would estimate at least 70 percent of the time, people with or without narcotics on their person or in their house would let us in and search. Those with dope would be confident they had their stash well hidden (usually not).

46

I wasn't into good cop–bad cop scenarios. But sometimes people pissed me off, and the bad cop did come out. I can be home all day with my kids and neighbors and act quite properly and speak decently. Then the minute I walk in the front doors at the police station, depending on the situation, the F bombs start flying.

Before my wife and I were married and working narcotics together, we had a bad guy in an interview room. We made our grand entrance in an attempt to get a confession about some dope deal, but this dough head gets all cocky with me, acting like he's the one in charge.

Without hesitating, I said, "Listen the fuck up here, motherfucker, get one fucking thing straight. In this room, I'm the fucker and you're the fuckee."

By now, my partner could hardly control herself, laughing at all the testosterone in the room.

During my narcotics days, I worked primarily with the same two officers and sergeant the entire time. When a group stays together that long, they must first get along and, second, be productive. These two officers were Brandon Sweet and Jimmy Quinn. The other two slots in our unit would switch every so often, based on transfers and promotions.

Brandon Sweet was about five years older than I and had been in the narcotics unit for three or four years before me. He was a quick talker and a hard worker, who always had a perfect tan and perfect slicked-back hair. If I had a dollar for every hair joke that was made to Brandon during my career, I would be a rich man today.

Jimmy Quinn was a tall, muscular black guy with huge hands. These hands served him well when he was a college football receiver. Jimmy had a knack for street talk and was able to work undercover with great expertise. I also had great admiration for Jimmy because he was raised in the inner city, but overcame any odds against him by becoming a college graduate and a police officer. On more than one occasion, I entrusted my life to these two guys, and they will forever be my friends. Both Brandon Sweet and Jimmy Quinn had narcotics expertise, experience, and documentation skills that would be used later in the triple homicide case.

Our leader of this narcotics crew was a guy named Tommy Stash. He was a career drug guy who became a policeman when he was nineteen years old. That's even younger than the legal drinking age, as if the system was saying, "Here's a gun. Go make good decisions, kid." Well he must have made some good decisions because he was running one of the most fast-paced dope-busting crews. Stash had two demands on us: do good, honest police work and eat a big dinner early so nobody's hungry later at night when we're serving warrants.

Stash was a great mentor for me. We probably agreed on every aspect of policing except one. He loved the media. He was always giving press briefings. At times, it seemed as if I would see him all night at work and all day on TV or hear him on the radio.

My greatest seizure during my narcotics career was not a getaway car, not a house filled with dope, not even a large sum of drug money. My greatest seizure, by far, was meeting my wife, after her arrest at a search warrant.

A trophy picture taken after the first multi-pound undercover cocaine buy in Omaha, in the mid-1990s. From left to right: Curtis Warbox, me holding the cocaine and buy money, Jimmy Quinn, Sgt. Tommy Stash, and Harley Blair.

No, that's a joke! My wife was also a narcotics officer on our crew for a couple of years. Rae is by far the most wonderful woman I have ever known. She is a loving, caring, wife and mother, but she is also tough, or at least she likes to think she is, especially after she participated in modern warrior classes, learned the critical pressure points to drop a guy in his tracks, and she practiced these techniques on me—even in the front yard much to horror of our neighbors.

She gets it. She has a common sense approach, knows life priorities better than I do, keeps our family together, and keeps me grounded when I get too involved in cases or projects. Every day she makes me feel special, which is the greatest feeling in the world.

Narcotics crew, late-1990s, from left, back row, Brandon Sweet, Jimmy Quinn, Curtis Warbox, Sgt. Tommy Stash; front row, my wife Rae and me.

It was during these narcotics days that my ability to develop and cultivate informants got better and better. One investigation, for example, began with a simple phone call regarding a complaint of narcotics activity at a house. My wife (not then) and I prematurely did a "knock and talk" on a suspect in the house.

As it turns out, this night was the day before Halloween. We knocked on the door and identified ourselves as police officers, but the suspect did not believe we were real cops. He thought it was a joke being played on him by some of his friends and basically told us, "Get the fuck off my porch" and tell so-and-so, "that's really funny." We had no recourse and had to leave because we had no probable cause. I was pissed because this guy didn't believe us and kind of punked us out.

The next morning, I do what we should have done from the beginning and tried to develop our own probable cause. One way to do this was to search the suspect's trash, looking for evidence of narcotics activity. Any trash set out at the curb is fair game. No search warrant needed.

As luck would have it, the next morning was this guy's trash day. I hooked up with the trash truck the following morning. We cleared out the hopper on the truck so the back end was empty. I rode on the truck as it made its usual route through the neighborhood and picked up the suspect's trash, and then the garbage truck guys drove me around the corner to my car. I put all the suspect's trash into clean bags and searched it at the police station.

I found some marijuana seeds in the trash along with rotten food, used condoms, and dirty magazines. Bingo! Probable cause to get a search warrant. By the time our shift was starting, not even sixteen hours later, we had our signed search warrant and we were back at his house.

"Who's the real cop now, asshole?" I was saying as I knocked the door off its hinges.

During the search, we found around $150,000 in cash and a kilo of cocaine. This guy could not wait to talk, and he gave up his supplier quickly. We then developed a case on his supplier, who ultimately rolled over on his supplier, going several tiers up the chain in this cocaine conspiracy.

When we developed information that the highest guy in Omaha was connected to a high-level cocaine distributor in Las Vegas, we actually developed probable cause and wrote a state-authorized wiretap that led to the indictment of both the highest level Omaha drug dealer and the Las Vegas source who was identified as Bandido Bucco.

As I began to research Bucco with the Las Vegas Police Department, I was told that he also had a father in the Las Vegas area who was documented as an associate of a mob family from New York. After this father had served time in prison for murder in the 1950s, the mob set him up in Las Vegas at a casino. The father, whose name was Bandido Bucco, Sr., was a doorman at a high-stakes poker game and reportedly got a thousand-dollar tip from every player that entered the room.

As the investigation continued, we got arrest warrants for everybody, including the Las Vegas supplier, Bucco (the son, not the dad). I actually went to Las Vegas to arrest Bucco and serve a warrant on his residence. During this warrant, we found all kinds of nice big-boy toys: wave runners, four wheelers, a huge boat.

Just to be thorough during this investigation, I made contact with the father (the mob murderer). This gentleman had a beautiful home and a beautiful wife half his age. I introduced myself and talked about the investigation, asking him if he purchased any of the items that were recovered from his son's property, hoping to avoid a later claim that those items were not proceeds from the narcotics operation.

This guy was totally cool. "Hell, no, I did not buy him that stuff, I don't go for that drug business," he told me.

All of the court proceedings were held in Omaha in the federal courthouse in our jurisdiction. As any good father would, Bandido Bucco, Sr., showed up to every hearing in support of his son. I thought that was pretty upstanding of him.

During this time in my life, I would usually bring my four-year-old daughter, Jocie, to court with me to save money on a babysitter. In county court, I always had one of the clerks in the County Attorney's office watch her when I testified. But this was federal court, so I would have to have Jocie sit in the gallery—no babysitter was available.

During the next several months and through multiple hearings, Bandido Bucco, Sr., and Jocie became friends as they sat in the front row of the gallery together. It was crazy walking out of the courthouse with him saying to my daughter, "See ya later, Jocie," in that gravelly mobster kind of dialect.

I joke with people to this day that with one phone call, if somebody messes with my daughter, I could have them whacked by my mob connection. But again, it all goes back to interpersonal skills and dealing with people. This case also demonstrates the development of a narcotics case using multiple investigative tactics.

Around 2002, a captain in the Criminal Investigations Bureau started a new unit called Special Investigations, which was for cases of his selection that he did not want going to specific units. That's when I was recruited to report to Sgt. Harry Bogowski. I had never worked with him, but had heard he was very intense and was a veteran homicide detective who worked some high profile cases in the past.

Sgt. Bogowski and I hit it off right away. He had a lifelong love of baseball and so did I. He was an old-school homicide detective who was thorough to the tenth degree in the way he investigated. I, being from a narcotics background, was more creative (I'd like to think) in my investigations, so once the evidence to arrest was obtained, the arrest was made, and we went on to our next investigation.

An example of my creative investigative nature can be exemplified in the second narcotics wiretap that I wrote. In this case, the target under investigation was a twenty-one-year-old guy who owned his own house, multiple cars, had a full-time job as an electrician's apprentice, and sold pounds of both cocaine and methamphetamine. This guy also had a hot, bodybuilding girlfriend, who also worked full-time, but was fully aware of the narcotics activity and assisted to a small degree in the conspiracy.

This guy also maintained about six other girls on the side—he was a machine. He would go from work to drug deal to girl after girl. It was exhausting just watching and listening to him. He would have one girl leaving his house as his main girlfriend was pulling up the street. These girls' cars would actually pass each other right in front of the house.

Here's where it gets creative. When the investigation was coming to an end, search warrants were written on all locations where probable cause was developed during the entire wiretap for evidence of the drug conspiracy. I had made a cassette tape of at least ten phone calls where this guy was all "kissy and goosey" with other girls. When we hit his main house with the search warrant and his girlfriend was secured at this location, she was taken into a room where the tape of her boyfriend getting romantic with all the other girls was played. She got redder and redder and more pissed with each passing second. Before the tape was even halfway through, she became state's witness number one.

Now that I was assigned to this new special investigations unit, our worlds would meet: the narcotics-type investigation, which was often offensive and creative, joined forces with the homicide-type investigation, which is more responsive with follow-up. I definitely learned during these early cases in the special investigations unit under Sgt. Bogowski the art and skill of patience and thoroughness, but I still always tried to keep that creative edge from my narcotics days.

After a year, Sgt. Bogowski was recruited back to the homicide unit, and he was trying to get several people whom he had worked with in the past to go with him. I had my choice now: go back to narcotics, where my comfort level was high, but the cases were all the same, in general, or go with him to homicide, where the stakes were much higher and the success ratio did not look all that promising. It was a tough decision but, deep down, I knew I wanted to take a crack at homicide.

8
DEATH SQUAD

My anxiety was high and my apprehensions were extreme about working in the homicide unit for many reasons. For the first time in my career, I was actually going to be working during the daytime and at central police headquarters, which meant that I would run into upper command officers. These upper command officers are generally full of politicking and self-promoting. In reality, it's about a fifty-fifty mix—half were good cops and still "got it" (the idea of putting the bad guy in jail), but the other half I tried to stay away from. Most of them didn't know the difference between handcuffs or a hand job.

My second apprehension was that I was a horrible typist, so when I worked in narcotics, I would dictate my search warrants to a typist. I had heard that the detectives in the homicide unit or at central police headquarters had to type their own search warrants. That scared me more than being shot at. So prior to accepting this new position, I negotiated with Sgt. Bogowski who assured me that I would have access to a secretary for dictating my search warrants.

Well, in my first hour, sitting at my new desk in the homicide unit, I literally had nothing to do, so I walked up to the unit secretary and introduced myself to her.

"Hi. I'm new here. I don't know what the heck's going on," I told her. "If you can help me out."

"Guess what," Robin said. "It's my first day too."

From that time on, Robin and I hit it off and had a great working relationship. The homicide secretary has a huge job keeping track of reports and entering them into the homicide books—the murder books, monstrously thick three-ring binders. Information is constantly flowing from detectives' dictation to the typing pool generating reports and then into the books. Robin's job was critical, and she was magnificent at it.

Other crew members included Padre Thorton, a twenty-three-year veteran, who had worked a majority of his career in the youth services unit and, during that time, had investigated several child abductions and murders. A tall guy with thick gray hair, Padre had a deep, scratchy voice that came off sincere, not gruff. In the interview room, suspects always ended up making a connection to Padre by often admitting to horrific crimes because of his fatherly tone.

At the same time my triple murder was being investigated, Padre was the lead investigator on a high-profile case in which an adolescent girl was slain and dumped in a desolate park near the Missouri River. It was a pressure-cooker of a case because the media were focused on Padre's case, not the triple murder, and he solved the case and brought the murderer to justice.

Sitting in the desk directly next to me was Isadore Demann, who had been assigned to the homicide unit for a couple of years. Isadore was an ex-college football lineman with a shaved head, but always had his suits pressed and his appearance flawless. Isadore was known for his ability to interact and interview suspects, often gaining confessions and was very thorough in his documentation skills.

Next was Sammy "Scrap Iron" Golic, a guy who, at first, was hard to figure out, but I quickly realized he was dedicated and hard-working and definitely had a gift for the technical stuff, like cell phones and computers. Often, I would look over at him sitting at his desk, and he would be rocking in his chair, like Dustin Hoffman in *Rainman,* just pondering some piece of evidence or records. He was a huge asset in several investigations. He earned the nickname "Scrap Iron" because he did an American Wrestling Association imitation of George "Scrap Iron" Gadaski.

Last was Roscoe Hogan, who was hard-working and willing to do anything to get the job done. He was my partner on several murders and will always be like a brother to me. Roscoe had a loud, boisterous voice and was definitely the life of any party, never being seen without two beers in his hands, if enjoying cocktails after work. Often, without any notice, Roscoe would just grab you in a big bear hug, squeezing so tight you wanted to cry, then set you down, saying, "I love you, man."

Roscoe's biggest asset was his memory. During an investigation, he could remember little facts without having to refer to reports or could at least make reference to where pieces of information were gained during the investigation so they could quickly be referenced.

The command staff consisted of Sgt. Harry Bogowski and our Lieutenant, N.S. Boss, who was a straight-talking, no sugar-coating guy, who probably lacked some people skills, but was extremely smart and knowledgeable about the investigative process. He always got the job done, and that's why I liked him.

Now the stage is set. I'm just waiting for my first murder. I was hoping the first one might be some type of domestic violence situation with the suspect on the scene still holding the murder weapon. No such luck.

My second night on the job, I went to bed around 9:30. About thirty minutes later, the phone rang. It was Sgt. Bogowski saying, "Bo, we got one. Double murder. Nineteenth and Drexel. Vehicle shot numerous times.

Four people in the car. Two are dead. Go to Central. You're interviewing one of the survivors."

At central station, I ended up interviewing a fifty-five-year-old Hispanic guy named Marcos Garcia. He told me about his involvement in an international marijuana distribution ring and how he was in the Omaha area with the other parties in the vehicle to collect money for an outstanding debt, but they were ambushed in lieu of payment.

Holy shit! I'm out of the narcotics unit and in the homicide unit, and I got a statement that incriminated twelve different people in a drug conspiracy resulting in murder.

At my first briefing, I tried to sell Sgt. Bogowski on a narcotics conspiracy case to develop the murder case and that's what we methodically did, federally indicting a bunch of people on numerous charges, ultimately developing witnesses that enabled us to prosecute the murder. This investigation took almost a year to complete, ending with a two-week jury trial. Three people were found guilty of first-degree murder.

This confused me because, on TV, it generally takes the police forty-eight hours to investigate, catch, and have the trial, convicting the bad guys; however, my first investigation took well over forty-eight *weeks.*

This same type of investigation happened to me again on a home invasion murder of a white, college-aged guy. I was assigned to interview the surviving roommate, who was in the house at the time of the home invasion and heard the struggle between his roommate and the intruders, which ended with multiple gunshots being fired and his roommate being murdered.

During my six-hour interview with the roommate, he admitted to being a marijuana dealer at a multi-pound level. He admitted to me that there were five pounds of marijuana hidden in the clothes washer in the laundry room of the house.

Handling the crime scene was Sgt. Bogowski and Roscoe Hogan.

I called Sgt. Bogowski and asked him, "Did anyone look in the clothes washer yet?"

To which the sergeant replied, "We're about outta here. We've been over this place a couple times."

"But has anyone checked the washing machine?" I insisted.

To appease me, Sgt. Bogowski was still on the phone as he walked to the laundry room.

I could literally hear him crap his pants when he located the five pounds of marijuana and growled, "Fuck, Bo, are you kidding me."

Roscoe and I were assigned the follow-up on this investigation. Through the investigative process, we arrested many individuals on narcotics-related charges and developed a witness that led to the conviction of one gang member for this home invasion robbery and murder.

The marriage of narcotics investigations and homicide investigations was becoming very fruitful. Instead of cultivating informants like in narcotics cases, we were now cultivating witnesses in murder cases.

Detective Sam "Scrap Iron" Golic actually made a nameplate for my desk that labeled my own personal unit as the "Narco-Homicide Unit." How true that turned out to be when I caught the case of the three bodies burning.

9
PUTTING THE HORSE BEFORE THE CARTEL

We knew the names of our three victims, but we needed to know what they were really about. *Why did someone kill them?*

The next phase of the investigation involves the victimology, which is simply researching the victims and learning as much as possible about their activities and background. To do this, we conduct interviews with family and friends and research old police reports, income taxes, or any source available that would provide background about these victims.

We made many contacts at the hotel where the two half-brothers stayed. During these interviews with hotel employees, we determined that Ricardo "Richie" Gomez and Barry Willis had stayed at the hotel for three days before their bodies were found. There were no phone records connected to the hotel room that we could follow up, which is not surprising because these days everyone uses their cell phones.

When I talked with the afternoon front desk clerk, she said, "The bigger of the two guys staying in that room [Richie Gomez] would often come down to the lobby and sit on the couch," and pointed to a couch in a grouping around a fireplace. "It looked like something was on his mind, as if he was worried about something."

"Did he say something to you," I asked, "that made you think this?"

"No, it was just a feeling I got by the way he acted," she said.

This by itself is an interesting fact that we hope can be explained later as the investigative process moves ahead.

We also were able to verify through airline flight records when both Barry and Richie arrived in Omaha. Through conversations with family members, we found out that Floreno Gonzalez arrived in Omaha by vehicle after receiving a ride from a family friend or associate in Denver, Colorado. It was still unclear as to why these three guys were together at the time they were murdered.

Detective Isadore Demann was still busy with the crime scene and autopsy follow-up, so Sgt. Bogowski assigned Roscoe and me to do interviews in Arizona. Within the first couple weeks after the murder, Roscoe and I were in

Phoenix two different times trying to talk with as many people as possible to get to know our victims.

After arriving in Phoenix, our first goal was to meet with the twin brother of Barry Willis who was also the half-brother of Ricardo "Richie" Gomez. He was identified as Carlos Willis. We talked with Carlos by phone. Even though he agreed to meet with us prior to our arrival, he was very apprehensive and hesitant to actually make contact with us once we arrived in Phoenix.

"We're in town. Where can we come meet you?" I wanted to know.

"I can't meet you right now," he said.

"Bullshit. It's your brother who got killed, and I just flew halfway across the country, so figure out where we're going to meet," I said.

Eventually, a negotiation was made with Carlos to meet at a safe location, which he picked and ended up being Luke Air Force Base, just outside Phoenix. He was a member of the Air Force Reserve. It was the only place he felt comfortable. The MPs let us on base with our police IDs with no problem.

We actually met at a cafeteria on the base. We sat in a booth across from Carlos Willis. It was creepy looking at him because he was identical to his brother, Barry, whom we had seen dead and burned just a week or so earlier.

During this interaction with Carlos, his actions and movements were unusual. We picked up signs of fear and paranoia. He asked for our police IDs, trying to verify that we were actually investigators with the Omaha

Police Department. Eventually, Carlos became mildly accepting of us.

"I'm worried that they're going to come after me," he said concerned for his own safety. "People from the 'other side' who were out millions of dollars may hold me responsible for my brother's lost money and dope."

This term, *other side,* confused Roscoe and me, so we asked Carlos about it, who explained the other side was people from Mexico. I took that to mean a drug cartel from Mexico.

Carlos went on to explain that he and his twin, Barry, and their half-brother, Richie, have the same mother, whom he identified as Maria Moreno. Carlos said Richie was born in Mexico, but came to the United States with their mother, who married his and Barry's father, having him and his brother after they married. Carlos told us Richie and his mother never became U.S. citizens.

During this entire conversation and interaction with Carlos, he leaned forward and talked in a very quiet voice, always looking around, fearful that he was being watched, even though we were on a secure military base.

Carlos explained that Richie graduated a few years earlier from Arizona State University and had a degree in business accounting, but he could not get a real job because he was not a U.S. citizen. Because of this situation, Richie had to make contacts in Mexico through old relationships their mother had with marijuana dealers. Through these contacts, Richie was working his way up the ranks in a Mexican drug organization.

When asked at what level Richie was in this organization, Carlos said Richie was organizing deals all over the United States, in New York, Pennsylvania, Alabama, and Atlanta, along with Phoenix. Specifically, Carlos said the deal taking place in Omaha was a large amount of marijuana, of which millions of dollars were not accounted for, and this Mexican drug organization was at a loss for the marijuana and the money.

Carlos stated he had received one call from a guy, who indicated he was associated with this drug organization, and they wanted to meet with him, but he said he did not go to this meeting, fearing he would be killed, and that was why he had been acting so paranoid. Carlos said he has not even been to his own house since the murders because he is fearful the Mexican drug organization is watching his house.

Carlos told us he has had telephone contact with a guy who lives in Phoenix, around Seventy-fifth and Camelback, who has the street name of "Bully," and during this conversation, he learned that Bully was getting his marijuana from Richie.

We figured we needed to talk with Bully for more information about who the connection was for the drug deal that led to the murders in Omaha.

Carlos said during his conversations with Bully, he was trying to get as much information as he could because he needed to know this information for a couple reasons. First, he wanted to provide the information to law enforcement, and second, he thought he needed the information in case he was ever captured by the Mexican drug organization and they wanted information on what had happened in Omaha.

Bully described the connection in Omaha as a black dude who went by the street name of "Shine," Bully had said to Carlos, and Shine was somehow associated with a barber shop. However, Carlos said he did not know if the barber shop was in Phoenix or in Omaha.

Carlos was now becoming more comfortable with us and continued to speak more freely. Richie was in Omaha, he said, to collect money for a very large shipment of marijuana—several million dollars. Carlos said his twin, Barry, only went along to keep Richie company while he waited for the money.

Carlos also described how his last contact with Barry was at around ten o'clock the night before the bodies were discovered. During this conversation, everything seemed to be normal. Barry said he would be home in a day or so, but there was no mention or feeling that anything was wrong.

"So who's the guy that's with your brothers?" we asked, referring to Floreno Gonzalez, the dead guy who had been wearing cowboy-style clothing.

"I don't know who that dude is. I've been trying to figure that out myself. But I believe that he's with the cartel, and he was there to make sure everything went smooth," Carlos told us.

Also contacted on our trip was Barry Willis's girlfriend, Courtney Vasquez. She was a twenty-year-old, attractive, soft-spoken, young Hispanic woman, who was still somewhat in a state of shock about the murders.

Courtney described how Barry had only recently begun to do more things with his half-brother, Richie. She explained how Richie just recently bought Barry a second cell phone. We asked Courtney why Barry would need a second cell phone, but she did not have an answer, whether that was really from not knowing or not wanting to acknowledge that Barry was starting to go down the wrong path in the drug world.

"When was your last contact with Barry?" we asked her.

"I know exactly when it was," she said holding up her cell phone. Courtney told us it was at 9:00 p.m., which would make it 11:00 p.m. in the Midwest.

"He said he was at a drug store shopping for tape and a calculator," she remembered. "He talked as if everything seemed normal. He said he was going to be home in a few days. He didn't sound worried."

"Why would Barry buy tape and a calculator?" I wanted to know.

"For counting money and taping it up," she didn't hesitate.

I'm sure Courtney had a very good idea about what Barry's and Richie's activities were in the narcotics world.

Shortly after the interview we received Barry's credit card details from the credit card company in the mail, which verified a small purchase at 11:30 p.m. from a midtown Walgreen's. The actual transaction was researched at the specific drug store around Seventy-Second Street, which detailed that three items were purchased: a roll of tape, a soda pop, and the letters "c-a-l-c." The store was not sure what the abbreviations stood for because it was under a miscellaneous UPC code, but I'm pretty confident, based on Courtney's statement, he was purchasing a calculator.

At this point, loads of paper start flying—from detectives to typists to me. I kept my own copies of reports, historical phone records, and every scrap of evidence we had generated. I told the unit, "The only way we're gonna be successful and not get overrun with all this bullshit is to stay organized. That's the key to success." I just knew this case was going to produce massive amounts of paperwork.

After that, I was incessantly teased in the unit about my profound statement: "Organization is the key to success." But it really is true. Many cases fall apart because detectives aren't organized.

We had received a phone call from a woman claiming John Doe 3, Floreno Gonzalez, was her husband, and shortly after that call, she simply showed up at the police station along with a three-year-old girl and a man who was thought to be her brother.

Floreno, she said, through a police officer interpreter, had been involved with large-level marijuana suppliers in Mexico. She said during a couple of Floreno's last transportation deals, the loads were somehow lost and Floreno was held accountable for these losses, and he was now in great debt to the Mexican suppliers.

Floreno's wife, a rough-looking Hispanic woman about thirty-five years old and who looked much older, told us that a deal was worked out to remove this debt, where Floreno was to come to Omaha, make contact with Richie Gomez, and make sure everything went smoothly in the collection of money.

She provided us photos of him, but we couldn't identify John Doe 3 specifically because the fire had burned his face so badly. So we obtained a DNA sample by taking a swab from inside the mouth of their young daughter. Weeks later, the DNA confirmed John Doe 3 as Floreno Gonzalez.

At this point, we know who the dead guys are, but still we don't know why they were killed, and we're still a long way from figuring out who did it.

10
YOU BIG BULLY

"Bully." Roscoe and I needed to put a real name to this nickname—the Phoenix guy Carlos Willis said might have firsthand knowledge of "Shine"—the black guy from Omaha.

To connect the dots, we needed the assistance of some local Phoenix police officers. We had already developed contacts with the local authorities, advising them that we were in town. They agreed to help us if we needed anything.

We hooked up with two gang detectives in the Phoenix Police Department named Joshua Howard and Adam Morris. They entered the nickname "Bully" into their databases and did, in fact, come up with a name of Jesse Romo at an address in the area of Seventy-Fifth and Davonshire, which was only one block from the area of Camelback, where Carlos thought Bully lived.

We gained as much information about Jesse as we could from the local authorities, who advised that Jesse and his brother Adam Romo and three other individuals named Derek Malo, Kenny Boston, and Beto Rojas were identified in a crew that was involved in home invasion robberies and drug dealing. We asked the local Phoenix gang cops to get us as much information as they could on this crew so we could start running backgrounds on them and try to determine if they were in the Omaha area during the time of our murder.

We also asked for the quickest way to get to Jesse "Bully" Romo's home address, so we could make an attempt at interviewing him. It was Roscoe's and my belief that if we played up the fact that we were just trying to avenge his friend Richie's murder, he may cooperate with us.

Joshua Howard and Adam Morris were very cooperative with us in providing the information, but I sensed that they did not have a lot of confidence in a couple of Midwest cops' ability to deal with Arizona dough heads, but they graciously assisted as we went to Bully's house in an attempt to get more information.

Roscoe and I walked up to the front door of a single-story, stucco-style house in a middle-income neighborhood in Phoenix. The residence itself appeared to be well kept and did not lead us to believe that its occupants were gang members or drug dealers involved in home invasion activities.

We knocked on the door. Within a few seconds, a young Hispanic kid in his early twenties, who definitely could have been Jesse Romo, based on the mugshot photograph we had been shown by the local authorities, opened the door. This guy was friendly and listened to Roscoe and me as we identified ourselves, explained who we were, and what our purpose was for being there regarding the murder of Ricardo "Richie" Gomez.

He said, "Bully's my brother. I don't know where he's at. I haven't seen him in weeks."

The three of us were still standing at the door. Then he identified himself as Adam Romo, but friends called him "Zeke." Adam said he had heard about the murders, and people in Arizona who knew Richie were very upset. Zeke then invited us into the house and indicated he would speak with us, telling us everything he knew regarding Richie.

Over the next hour and a half, Zeke incriminated himself in numerous drug deals involving Richie, himself, and a black guy who went by the street name of Shine who was from Omaha. Zeke then described a second black guy who was always with Shine who went by the nickname "Nephew," but added that Shine was definitely the one in charge.

Zeke continued, "If you need more exact details about the black dudes from your town, you need to talk to Roy and K.B., because it was actually K.B. who introduced Shine to us all in the beginning." These names mentioned by Zeke directly correlated with the names we had already received as documented associates from the Phoenix detectives. K.B. was Kenny Boston and Roy was Derek Malo.

This information was huge with more leads to follow, except our flight back home was scheduled to leave the next morning, and we really wanted to get back to Omaha because both Roscoe and I had left our wives with a houseful of children to deal with and our own survival depended on getting back home on time.

We consulted with the Arizona detectives, who provided some background information on some of our new parties of interest. We learned that Derek Malo, a/k/a (also known as) Roy, was in jail on a robbery charge, and Kenny Boston, a/k/a K.B., was currently on the run with an outstanding warrant for attempted murder because he had shot a guy six times over some minor altercation.

What was even more interesting about the incident with Kenny Boston's shooting was it had occurred on May 4, which was the day *before* the three bodies were located, so, in essence, that provided Kenny a fairly good alibi for the murders that happened in Omaha.

Even though our flight was scheduled to leave the following day around noon, Roscoe and I wanted to take a shot at Derek Malo because we knew where he was (in jail) and his information could be very valuable.

Roscoe and I arranged for an interview room that morning before our flight. This actually was a pretty risky move because if Derek did become cooperative with us and started talking, that conversation could go on for hours. If that happened, we could miss our flight, but it was a risk we were willing to take.

We did end up meeting face to face with Derek Malo in the Maricopa County Jail, which is the famous correctional facility run by the infamous sheriff of Maricopa County where the inmates have to wear pink jumpsuits and underwear. During our conversation with Derek, it was apparent that he was playing a tactical game with us, definitely feeling us out, trying to determine the best deal he could get by cooperating with us.

In all reality, we had no bargaining power for any charges for which he was incarcerated. We separated on good terms with Derek that day, telling him that we would give it our best effort to solve our case without him.

In the parking lot, I told Roscoe, "Fuck him. We'll indict his ass based on what Zeke told us and then we'll see if he wants to talk."

It was now time to get home, back to the Midwest, think about what we had learned, research the nickname Shine, research all the phone numbers we learned from the interviews that were associated with our victims, trying to associate them with any local telephone numbers in our town, and wait for Kenny Boston to get arrested on his attempted murder warrant.

It was also apparent that many players were going to be involved at many different levels in this conspiracy. We created an association chart to visualize all the people involved because, as the number of players grew, we didn't want to overlook or forget anybody.

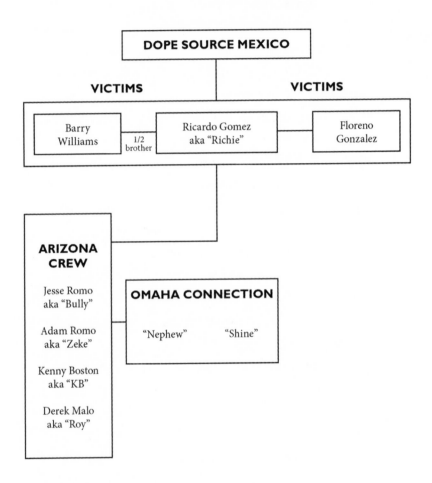

11
NICKNAMES BUT
NO REAL NAMES—YET

After returning to Omaha, we briefed Sgt. Bogowski so the lead investigator, Isadore Demann, could have all the information we had gathered.

"Bo, this case has got you written all over it," the sergeant said to me. "You want it? You got it." Because this was a dope deal gone bad, and I came from a narcotics background and had experience solving dope-related murders by indicting all conspirators, it was Demann's lucky day.

I was thinking, *This case is a monster and probably a loser. No, no, no.* But my voice said, "Yes, sir."

Our next move, we told him, was figuring out who these local guys were. We were looking for a black guy with the nickname of Shine and a guy he ran with who was called Nephew. The physical description of each was very vague: black males, clean cut, between six feet and six feet two, with Shine being about 220 pounds, and Nephew being a little bit thicker. Could have been anybody.

Within our local metro police department, there are several ways through various databases to search for people only by their nicknames. These systems included a Field Observation Card System, which is a program where every significant contact an officer has with a person on the street is entered onto a Field Observation Card. These cards are then downloaded into a database with such information as the location of the contact, nicknames, and people who are present during the contact.

As this database grows larger and larger, it produces valuable information that can be learned about people over time: who their associates are, vehicles they are using, areas where they congregate, and types of crimes they are involved in.

We checked this system. No hits. No correlations found with either nickname of Shine or Nephew.

A second source of information is a computer program that searches all typed reports within the metro area police department for key words or phrases. Again, with the key words of *Shine* or *Nephew,* there was never any word association that actually tied either name to any specific individuals.

This information was passed on to all units within the metro area police department who had contact with street sources to determine if anyone had ever heard of Shine or Nephew. The results were negative. We still had nothing on their identities.

The busy work continued, first, by researching and verifying the information that had already been received—specifically, the information that Carlos Willis provided about his mother (and the mother of Ricardo "Richie" Gomez and Barry Willis) being an illegal alien. We checked with the Border Patrol and Customs. They confirmed that not only was the mother an illegal alien, but she had been arrested on several occasions for transporting quantities of marijuana across the border and deported just as many times for these incidents.

I kept in touch with Carlos Willis by phone. We tried to convince him to give us a contact number for his mother, but he said she was scared and hiding in Mexico, also fearful for her safety. However, she was arrested again trying to get back into the United States to attend the funeral of her two sons in Arizona. Because of her arrest, she never made it to the funeral.

She was detained in a small facility in New Mexico, pending her deportation. She had a history of drug smuggling herself. We thought she might have valuable information about the case.

Roscoe and I convinced our command to allow us to go there and make an attempt to speak with her regarding her knowledge of the murders. During our interview with her in New Mexico, she provided no information that was helpful in the murders at all. I felt only sorrow for her. She was a beaten and broken woman who had lived a hard life, and now her two sons had been murdered.

I believe she wanted to help us with the murder investigation, but she really had no direct knowledge that could be of any help. She did not know the specific dealings of her son, Richie Gomez, and who his customers were in Omaha. Also, out of self-preservation, she did not talk at all to us about who the Mexican sources were. I always felt sorry for her because of the burden she would always bear, being a piece of the puzzle that led to her sons being murdered. She had, no doubt, introduced her sons to the drug world.

Things were beginning to slow down. Leads were not coming in. Kenny Boston (the Arizona shooter who was on the run) had not yet been arrested, and Shine was not yet identified. If the case got slow, it could soon go cold, and detectives would be pulled away for other investigations. I didn't want that to happen—yet.

12
TEMPE STING—
IS THIS SOMETHING?

While waiting for information to come on Kenny Boston's status, a very interesting call came into the homicide unit. The caller was transferred to my desk.

My secretary Robin yelled across the homicide unit, "Hey, Bo, a cop is calling from Tempe saying he's got information about the triple."

Tempe is a suburb of Phoenix and is the city where Arizona State University is located.

The undercover narcotics cop from Arizona told me, "I'm making undercover buys from Beto Rojas. During one of the buys, he's talking about how he was in Omaha when three people get killed, and he escapes before he gets killed."

I'm thinking, *Holy shit, this guy could be a witness.*

This was a lot of information to digest quickly in this phone call. I asked what the status of his investigation was and if Beto was in custody yet. The undercover officer indicated the next delivery was scheduled to happen in a week, and it was for fifty pounds of marijuana. At that time, Beto was going to be arrested.

I asked this officer if he could forward me a copy of the conversation so that I could hear it for myself and present it to my command in an effort to sell one more trip to Arizona. I wanted to be on hand to interview Beto Rojas as soon as he was in custody. It took the undercover officer a little maneuvering within his own organization, but he pulled it off, and his supervisor granted the release of the tape to us prior to Beto's arrest. It was sent overnight, and I was listening to it within twenty-four hours of the phone call from Tempe.

When Roscoe Hogan, Sgt. Bogowski, and I listened to this tape, it was, without a doubt, a conversation in which Beto Rojas described that he was in Omaha at the time of the triple murder and escaped.

We waited for the week to pass and for the arrest of Beto Rojas to take place. Sometimes it is nice just to have things work out in your favor and that's exactly what happened. Also during this two- or three-day period, prior to Beto Rojas's arrest, I received a call from Joshua

Howard, the Phoenix gang officer, who advised that Kenny Boston had been arrested on his warrant.

Roscoe and I had now locked in our next trip to Arizona with these two specific interviews on the agenda: Beto Rojas, who may actually be an eyewitness to our triple murder, and Kenny Boston, who may be able to identify Shine.

Not only was I excited about this trip for the obvious investigative reasons, but one other thing I discovered on the first couple trips to Phoenix was an eatery called Waffle House. I had become addicted to it. There was no restaurant in Omaha that even came close to it. I could not wait to spend some per diem money on those sweet waffles.

When we arrived in Phoenix, we first met with the Tempe undercover officer who detailed his investigation on Beto Rojas. We then reconfirmed with the Arizona gang unit officers, Joshua Howard and Adam Morris, the association among all of the crew members in the Arizona gang, which included Jesse "Bully" Romo, Adam "Zeke" Romo, Derek "Roy" Malo, Kenny "K.B." Boston, and Beto "Junior" Rojas, who was actually at the lower end of the hierarchy of this gang.

Our interviews were set up. All Roscoe and I needed was a little something, a name or address in Omaha, to get us on the right trail to keep this journey going.

Our first interview was set up with Kenny "K.B." Boston. I should also mention that even though we had a successful interview with Adam Romo, our newfound friends in Arizona, Joshua Howard and Adam Morris, still did not think we had any chance at getting K.B. to even say hello to us, but Roscoe and I were still fairly confident.

We made arrangements with the Maricopa County Jail for an interview room, and upon arrival in the room, Roscoe and I sat down and waited for Kenny Boston to arrive. After only a few minutes, the door opened up and in walked a huge black guy, with muscles bulging in his arms, big chest, at least 300 pounds. He towered over us at six foot six—not an ounce of fat on him. This guy should have been a professional football player. If intimidation is part of any interaction in a jail interview, let me tell you, his physical presence was on the winning side.

The interview began with Roscoe and me making introductions and giving Kenny a description of our purpose and our goals. Kenny did not say anything for a long time. He just sat in his chair and listened to us talk.

This silence is not uncommon during these types of interviews. Here's what's taking place: the interviewee is assessing the detectives, listening to what they say, and analyzing if the detectives are any good and if there is any benefit for him to "play ball."

Eventually, I know that Kenny is going to ask, "What's in it for me?" And he did.

All I could offer at that time was my word that if he cooperated, I would convey that level of cooperation to his prosecutor on his pending case for consideration, but I, myself, could not promise him anything. I also tried to promote the theme that he must consider that his friend,

Richie Gomez, was executed and he could help bring that to justice.

These themes were restated and regurgitated at least a dozen times before Kenny finally said, "I like you guys. I'll tell ya."

Kenny then laid it out. He began by explaining that the guy from Omaha had the nickname of Shine, and he always had another guy with him whom he called Nephew. Kenny told us the association began by freak luck about a year before the actual murders.

Kenny said, "I was in a Circle K [convenience store] parking lot, hanging out and smoking a joint. This black dude comes up to me and said his name is Shine. We both started toking on the joint and talking shit. Shine says he's from Omaha, and he's looking for a hook-up."

Kenny described how they "kicked it" for a while, which is synonymous with hanging out with each other. Kenny said they were basically just feeling each other out, making sure neither one was somehow an informant or police officer or if they did become involved in some type of narcotics transaction, there would not be a rip-off.

When Kenny told us he was worried about being ripped off, I couldn't in my wildest dreams imagine anyone trying to rip this guy off, based on his physical size, not to mention my knowledge that he had busted off six rounds in a guy over some minor dispute. Pissing off Kenny Boston, I thought, would be like suicide.

Kenny said he was comfortable with Shine, so the next day he arranged for sixty pounds of marijuana to be delivered to Jesse and Adam Romo's house. Kenny indicated he was living at this house at the time because he did not have a place to stay. Jesse and Adam had an extra room.

Kenny said the transaction with Shine took place without any problems. At that time, Shine said he was looking to obtain much larger loads on a regular basis. Kenny told us this is exactly what happened, with the loads getting larger and larger and happening very frequently, maybe twice a month, sometimes getting as large as 600 pounds.

It was a perfect deal at the beginning, Kenny said, because everyone in his crew—Jesse, Adam, Derek, and himself—was plugged in with Richie and Richie was plugged in big with a Mexican source. Kenny said the price per pound was $300 for Shine during these initial deals, and Kenny himself received $50 of that sale price for each pound sold. Kenny indicated that life should have been good for everyone because all three were making money on the deal.

Incidentally, the price of marijuana in Omaha at this time was $1,000 to $1,200 a pound, depending on the quantity purchased and quality of the marijuana. Based on these numbers, the minimum profit for Shine on these deals would have been $700 per pound. Calculating just one 600-pound load would have produced a profit of $420,000, theoretically, depending on local negotiations. Regardless, even if it was a little less, that was still big money in the heartland.

To the best of his recollection, Kenny said he completed seven to eight deals in this same manner between Richie, himself, and Shine, but then things became a little twisted when Shine started talking to other members of the crew, specifically to Jesse and Derek, trying to negotiate better prices and, in a sense, going behind Kenny's back. Kenny said he knew there were a large number of deals that took place without him being involved, but he did not have a specific number.

Kenny also described how, two or three times, Richie was still at the house when Shine arrived to pick up the marijuana. He said Shine immediately picked up on the fact that Richie was the plug from Mexico and began trying to sell the idea of having a very large load delivered to Omaha, in lieu of Shine having to travel to Phoenix and then being responsible for the transportation of the marijuana back home.

Kenny then filled in big missing pieces: a big load that ended up in Omaha was negotiated in Atlanta, Georgia. Kenny described how Richie had a load going to Atlanta, but the intended recipients of this load could not accept the full load for some reason. My guess was that the original buyers had either been arrested or killed, but that was total speculation on my part.

So with this extra marijuana now in the Atlanta area, Richie asked Kenny if he had any contacts in Atlanta to unload this shipment of marijuana, which was already there.

Kenny then described how this request by Richie turned into almost a spring break party, with everyone from his crew going to Atlanta and partying, trying to find a customer for this load of marijuana. After several days, they had only found customers to accept maybe half of the available marijuana. They still had around 1,000 pounds of marijuana still on hand, so they decided to call Shine and see if he would come to Atlanta to buy this weed.

Shine accepted the offer and, within a day, the whole crew was in Atlanta, which included Richie Gomez, Jesse Romo, Derek Malo, Kenny Boston, Beto Rojas, Shine, and Nephew. Kenny then described how they all met at a famous strip club in Atlanta called Strokers, which is well-known because many professional athletes go there.

It was at a table in this strip club that the final negotiation took place between Shine and Richie for the large load to be brought up to Omaha. Kenny told us he did not hear all the specific details of the negotiation, but he did hear bits and pieces of it because they hashed it out right in front of him.

He said, "It wasn't any of my business. I didn't pay attention to the exact details, but I knew what they were talking about, and it was having a huge load delivered to Omaha straight from the cartel."

"When?" I asked him, and Kenny told us he thought it was two months before the murders—the middle of March.

This concept changed many variables. The marijuana would have had to travel a much greater distance across the country straight from Mexico to the Midwest, exposing the load to the danger of getting caught by authorities. To do this, the cost would have had to go up several hundred dollars per pound; however, for Shine, even with the extra cost, he had much less exposure and no transportation responsibility for getting the marijuana to Omaha. We now had a witness who actually saw the negotiations about the Omaha deal.

We still had the big question to answer, "Who was Shine?"

Kenny Boston only knew the nickname and didn't know what phone number Shine was using at the time and certainly did not have a good enough memory to remember the phone numbers of other people. Kenny said he couldn't even remember what cell phone company Shine was using at the time.

Roscoe and I next found Beto Rojas at another jail in the Maricopa County system. During this interview, it was obvious, just as Joshua Howard and Adam Morris had indicated, that Rojas was definitely at the lower end of the hierarchy within that crew. During this interview, it was quickly apparent that Beto did not have the "cojones" to be a big player in this game—specifically in the nasty world of gangland and dope dealing.

Beto did confirm that he was also in Atlanta with the other guys during the March meeting when Shine and all the other guys were present. I asked Beto why he talked about the murders in Omaha during his contact with the undercover officer, and Beto told me he was just talking shit, trying to make himself look like a player.

Roscoe and I also wanted to try to find Jesse "Bully" Romo while we were in Arizona to see what his statements would be regarding this investigation. Before we even had a chance to track him down, out of the blue, he called my cell phone. I'm sure he had to have received a call from Kenny or Beto, giving him a heads up that we were looking for him, and he must have decided it was better to meet with us rather than piss us off and risk a possible indictment on information we had already received.

When we did meet with Jesse, he was very cautious in his statements, although he did acknowledge that he was aware of all the drug transactions that took place in his house between Richie, Kenny, Derek, and Shine. Jesse told us that even though he was aware of them, he did not have anything to do with them. Jesse also confirmed that he was in Atlanta on the trip where the negotiations took place and specifically described the meeting at the strip club.

Roscoe and I then tried to come up with some way to justify a trip to Atlanta to get interviews at Strokers (and visit the local Waffle House), but even as creative as we were, we could not think of a way to pull it off and never even asked our command to send us to the strip club.

Once Roscoe and I arrived back home, I immediately began researching the trip to Atlanta by all of the people involved. It was not hard research. I had already subpoenaed every airline, checking to see if any of the crew from Arizona flew to Omaha at the time or shortly before the time of the murders.

Sure enough, everybody except Adam Romo flew from Phoenix to Atlanta in mid-March and none of them had flown to Omaha in May at the time of the murders. I also located flight records that showed Richie Gomez was in Atlanta during this same time in March.

Now I needed to verify that Shine and Nephew were there also, but I still did not know their names.

13
GIVE ME A BREAK

In every case, the good guys need a break, a piece of luck, something that is in no way the responsibility of good police work, just a twist of fate to break it open. I guess that's where the term *break* in police work comes from ("we caught a break") ("our big break was") ("all we need is a little break"). You hear this term all the time in police movies, in media, and in crime novels. Cops are always talking about the break.

Nearly six months had passed since the murders, and I had worked other murders. The case of the three bodies burning was basically dead in the water when all of a sudden, out of the blue, an evening shift homicide detective, Zachary George, who had been on the job about six years and had a strong New York accent, yelled over to my desk, "Bo, I got a felony assault shooting. This guy named Montel Jones got shot in the leg and he named his assailants as Shine, real name Preston Blade, and Nephew, real name Gaylan Green."

This was too good to be true. I was sure it had to be a practical joke—one of the guys was just trying to get me all riled up.

14
JOKERS WILD

Practical jokes were an integral part of my police career, not only on the giving end, but most certainly on the receiving end. From my early days in narcotics, practical joking was incorporated into the daily routines. I think it was almost subconscious as a stress reliever, even though, at that time in my life, I certainly did not feel like I had stress. Looking back, in reality, I'm sure we did. Our crew was serving no-knock search warrants at least four times a week, and we worked long night hours.

These practical jokes always kept us on our toes, especially at the narcotics office, which was its own separate facility, not associated with the police station at all. It was basically a fake business front in an industrial area to protect our undercover activities.

Some jokes were very predictable and not all that creative, but they were still funny. For example, it was not uncommon to enter into the work bay, where twenty-five detectives' desks would be lined up according to their unit, and find your desk completely gone. Just a big empty spot where you once sat.

Another joke that was always done happened to me after I would work out in this little makeshift exercise room that was built in the garage of this building. After a workout, I would go to a makeshift locker room and take a shower. Regularly, during this shower period, someone would sneak in and turn off the light switch, leaving me in complete darkness, naked in the shower, and the only switch to turn the lights on was twenty-five feet away by the door.

Remember I spoke of Brandon Sweet, one of my original narcotics crew members? He was the victim of many jokes because he had perfect hair. His hair was wavy and combed back—a cross between Elvis Presley and David Hasselhoff. At search warrants, he would be called to the bathroom of the house being searched as if there was some important piece of evidence that was found at this location. Instead, when he would arrive in the bathroom, we would have all the hair products from this house lined up for him to look at.

Often, we would set Brandon up regarding a contact he would have with a person. If a new officer or new informant was cultivated before Brandon was around, we would make sure this person would comment to Brandon as soon as he arrived about how beautiful his hair was.

The thing about these practical jokes, in reality, is that if someone is playing jokes on you, you actually know you fit in and you are well liked.

In the winter, it was normal to get called to a meeting location regarding what you thought was an upcoming search warrant or some type of deal getting ready to take place, but when you drove up, there would be nobody around. Then, eventually, one car would pull up and you would roll down your window to talk to the arriving crew member. Once your window was down, cops would jump out from hiding spots all around and bombard your open window with snowballs.

I was the victim of one of the best jokes one day when I arrived at work, sat at my desk, as normal, and checked my email. As I was doing this, I confided in Jimmy Quinn that I had taken my three-year-old daughter, Jocie, to the park that day and there was this twenty-two-year-old nanny also at the park, who was totally hot. I described how the nanny and I were sitting on the park bench and we had a really good conversation while the kids were playing. I also want to stress at this time that I was a single man.

After about an hour, I exchanged telephone numbers with the nanny. Jimmy listened to my story and said something like, "I hope it works out."

Well, no kidding, about an hour later, my phone rings and it's the nanny, but in this phone call, she was actually the naughty nanny, wanting to hook up as soon as we could. I fell right into her trap, talking smack and telling her I would try to get off work early that night. A few hours later, Sergeant Stash calls and says we have a search warrant to complete and set up a meeting spot for the briefing.

Once everybody was at the meeting spot, the sergeant said there was a recorded phone call the bad guy made to the informant regarding this deal. He then hit the play button on a recorder for everybody to listen to the call, but as we started listening, the conversation was me talking smack to the nanny.

For about a second I wanted to shoot somebody, but then I knew it was a superb practical joke. To this day, nobody will tell me who the female was who played the nanny, but it definitely was a good practical joke.

Some practical jokes were more outrageous than actually funny. There was a day shift narcotics officer who grew up on a farm and had a model of a John Deere tractor and trailer on his desk. For some reason, the night shift and day shift narcotics crews were battling in a joke war for a while, so for about a week, we had the narcotics dog handler take his dog out of the building near the end of the shift to relieve himself. We then put on rubber gloves, retrieved a portion of the dog poop, and put it in this guy's John Deere tractor trailer. That joke actually seemed funnier back then than it does now.

But my best gags came as a result of my diagnosis with testicular cancer. It sounds bad, but it turned out okay. So, in my battle, the doctors removed one of my "boys" (testicles). This, in turn, earned me such nicknames as "One Baller" and "Singlet," which I accepted with gratitude for one reason because I was actually still around to hear them.

Anyway, a lady police officer, who worked in the robbery unit at the time, asked me if I needed any beef because she raised a few head of cattle every year and sold off sides of beef. I accepted the offer. She added that she also had some young calves that were going to have their testicles removed. I asked her how big they were and she told me they were pretty good sized. I then asked her if I could have one to put on my desk. She said sure.

I went to the morgue, got a specimen jar full of formaldehyde, gave it back to the rancher cop and waited for my calf testicle. Within a few days, she brought back a jar with this monster testicle inside. I then displayed it on my desk, putting out the story that it was actually my ball and I had convinced the doctors to let me keep it. From that day on, people would always come to my desk checking out my giant testicle and always believing it was actually mine.

So for a detective to yell across the squad room that he had the names of the Omaha drug dealers, just like that, was surely somebody's idea of a whopper of a practical joke. I couldn't wait to find out who to pay back.

15
THE WHOLE TRUTH

Detective Zachary George was serious. He kept telling me, "Bo, I'm telling you, this is the truth. I'm not making this up." Finally, I actually believed and realized, *Holy shit! This was the big break.*

My list of things to do went from nothing to huge. I needed to interview the guy who got shot, Montel Jones; research the names of my possible suspects, Preston Blade (Shine) and Gaylan Green (Nephew). This research would include historical police reports and police contacts, telephone numbers, financial assets, taxes, vehicles owned, property owned, gang relations, friends, their daily routines, and flight histories to Phoenix and Atlanta.

The first order of business was to interview Montel Jones, and, fortunately, he was currently in jail on some unrelated petty crime. Also lucky for us, Montel was still pissed about being shot in the leg and didn't mind talking at all about the incident. At first, Montel had no problem describing the actual shooting, but was very vague on why he was shot in the first place.

"Bullshit, give it up. You know why you got shot," I said, thinking this fucker knew, but I'm still Mr. Nice Guy. "So tell me."

"They thought I was someone else, man. It was just a misunderstanding," he insisted.

"No way. Things don't happen that way. There's got to be a reason," I told him.

"Okay, all right, I'll tell ya," and then Montel said, it was common knowledge on the street that Preston "Shine" Blade and Gaylan "Nephew" Green were coming up big in the drug world and this was supported by their dramatic lifestyle improvements during the months prior to Montel being shot.

"They got nice shit there," he told us. "They're flashing money all around. They got a big plug somewhere."

Montel was a player. He lived a fast street life, always looking for the next angle to pull on someone. He was about thirty-seven, very skinny, with a rough beard, not well maintained. He told me he was able to figure out a house Shine was using as a stash house, so Montel enlisted the help of a friend, who was a career criminal named Wilson Mack—a guy with a history for doing armed robberies.

"We planned on doing a straight home invasion. We were gonna rob 'em and hold 'em at gunpoint and steal their shit," he said.

As they approached the house and knocked on the door, he said nobody answered, so they resorted to their fall-back plan of doing a normal burglary. As a result of the burglary, they found about 10 pounds of marijuana inside the house. Montel said he considered this a successful burglary because after the split between himself and Wilson Mack, each of them made a profit of $5,000 after selling the weed.

Montel told me this was all perfect in theory until he sold one of the pounds to one of Shine's cronies, who recognized the weed as some of Shine's that was ripped off during the burglary. I, myself, would not be able to tell the difference between one type of marijuana and the next, however, qualities do differ and people within that circle seem to know certain characteristics and traits of certain shipments of marijuana.

Regardless, word got back to Shine that Montel was responsible for his theft of 10 pounds of weed. Now, it would seem that just 10 pounds is not a great loss to Shine based on the large quantities of marijuana that were being brought into Omaha; however, it was not a matter of the size of the loss, it was actually a matter of street credibility, and Shine and Nephew needed to maintain that credibility. If they didn't, it would open the door for more people to attempt to rob and steal from them.

The best way to address the problem was for Shine and Nephew to find Montel Jones and shoot him, which is exactly what they did.

In the process of this shooting, they must have questioned Montel about who his accomplice was in that burglary because they later went after Wilson Mack. Montel never did make it to the end of this investigation. He was actually murdered a few months later in an unrelated incident.

The investigative process then continued with the interview of Wilson Mack, who was truly a career criminal. He had been in the joint several times. His latest problems stemmed from a series of convenience store robberies, where he would hog-tie the clerks in the back room, winning him the media name "The Hog-Tie Bandit."

After contact with him, in all actuality, it was kind of sad because he was a guy who actually had talent. He was a plumber by trade and had conversation skills that were very articulate, but he liked his drugs and women and the fast-paced life more.

Wilson Mack and I got along pretty well, although I had never come across him before in my career. We both knew many of the same people, which helped build the rapport when I began to talk to him.

Specifically, in regard to Shine and Nephew, Wilson said it was common knowledge on the street that these guys had been coming up quickly before those "three dead Mexicans" were found, and they were definitely coming up quickly afterward.

Wilson explained about the home invasion turned burglary, confirming what Montel Jones had said, but added that Montel had to have given his name to Shine and Nephew because a couple of weeks after Montel was shot, Wilson got word on the street that they were looking for him. Wilson said he avoided any altercations for a while, but Shine and Nephew finally tracked him down to a house where he was hiding out, which ironically, was near the ninth-grade school I was bused to many years earlier.

Wilson told me he was called by a friend, warning him that Shine and Nephew were on the block and coming for him. Wilson described how he went on the offensive, grabbed his SKS rifle, walked out the front door of the house he was hiding out in and watched them coming a half block away.

Wilson said he unloaded multiple rounds in their car and, in his words, "Those bitches got out and ran." Wilson said they fired a couple handgun rounds his way, but indicated he was not worried because he had superior fire power. Wilson stated he took off prior to the cops arriving but believed there had to be some police report made on the incident.

It took massive amounts of research, but sure enough, the incident was documented as a destruction of property because one of the houses on the street was hit by gunfire. During the investigation, nine rifle rounds were located and photographs were taken. That's pretty corroborative evidence to support Wilson's statement.

With the addition of several players and now having the identities of Shine and Nephew, it was time to update the association chart.

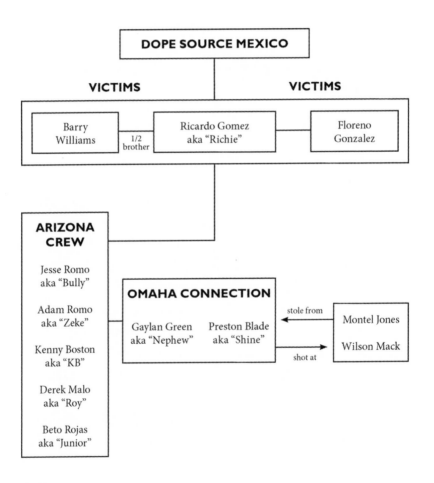

16
GOOD OLD GUMSHOEING

The marijuana dealers from Omaha were now identified. They were certainly suspects in relationship to the murders. They had been identified by name, but I definitely had not heard of either one of them, so the research phase began. Before this case would be over, we would accumulate over 13,000 pages of documents regarding past actions of Preston "Shine" Blade and Gaylan "Nephew" Green.

The research began simply enough with a search through the county mainframe computer, which lists basic information on people, such as their last known address, all of their police contacts, and whether they were a victim or suspect in a crime. This can then be followed up with a complete criminal history, which also checks people nationwide for their arrests and contacts. However, this search sometimes is not as accurate because the arrest information has to be put into the national system by the originating agencies, and some don't do that.

With these first simple scans, I saw some interesting entries on our new friends. First, Preston definitely was not shy about drug dealing. He had two prior crack cocaine entries with one conviction. This is not an uncommon observation—to have people arrested on more charges than they ever get convictions. This generally happens during the adjudication process when a plea bargain takes place and the suspect pleads to one charge and the other charges are dropped.

The benefits? For the prosecutor's office, a suspect pleading to lesser charges alleviates court or trial time. For the suspect, he only has one conviction, which can lead to less jail time.

Preston also had a pending charge of being a felon in possession of a firearm, resulting from a search of a vehicle he was in while sitting in the parking lot at a local hospital emergency room.

This tidbit of information was even more exciting when we learned that the search of this vehicle stemmed originally from a disturbance that happened inside the hospital emergency room area, where Preston wanted access to his friend in the emergency room—a guy with a gunshot wound to his arm.

Preston was kicked out of the hospital, and when a uniform patrol officer in a cruiser arrived, Preston was confronted in his vehicle. The cop found a handgun concealed under the driver's seat of Preston's vehicle.

Guess who Preston's friend was? The one with the gunshot wound to the arm? None other than Gaylan Green. During his interview with police regarding the gunshot wound to his arm, Gaylan claimed he had been shot by an unknown person for an unknown reason. When Gaylan came to the emergency room, he drove himself in a very nice, fairly new, black Chevy Z71 pickup truck with a tonneau cover over the bed of the truck.

Uniformed officers looked in the truck and saw a large amount of blood in the cab that was a result of his gunshot wound. These officers also opened up the tonneau bed cover on the truck and located four pounds of marijuana.

This was great information, but the marijuana was never used in any court proceeding because the search of the bed area of the truck was not warranted and could not be articulated as to why it was done in relationship to the shooting of Gaylan Green. So nothing ever resulted with the recovery of these four pounds of marijuana.

Those four pounds of marijuana meant a lot to me, however. It confirmed that the drug of marijuana had been identified by numerous people so far in this investigation and now linked to Gaylan. Plus, the truck seemed eerily similar to the one described by the neighbor in the wooded area—the driver who had face-to-face contact with a black truck at the intersection just to the south of where the bodies were located.

Even though no criminal prosecution ever resulted from that marijuana seizure, crime lab technicians were called to the hospital where they took pictures of the truck that night. This incident took place before the murders, thus giving us actual physical evidence or photos of the truck the way it looked then.

As a result of this initial information, I contacted Georgeann Goldstein of the County Attorney's Office. She had become my "go to" person for legal advice as it arose during my investigations. Georgeann had been the prosecutor on previous murder investigations I had completed, and I considered her to be the top dog in the County Attorney's Office. If this investigation ever evolved to a murder prosecution, it was my hope that she would be the prosecutor. Incidentally, she looked just like the actress Diane Lane from *The Perfect Storm*.

In making this contact with Georgeann, I requested that the County Attorney drop the pending felon in possession of a firearm charge against Preston. I wanted this charge dropped, which could always be re-filed at a later time, because I needed him to be out on the streets and feeling free. That way, I could start to stalk him, start watching his moves, and if he felt he had no pressure, he would be easier to watch.

This was so key in this case because we now had actually started to manipulate the psyche of Preston.

With the dropping of his charge, his confidence should have gone way up.

Another small prize came from a drunk driving arrest of Preston's, just eighteen days after the three bodies were discovered. As a result of this drunk driving arrest, about a half pound of marijuana, over $12,000 cash, and two cell phones were seized from him. These cell phones were booked into the police property room as personal property, but Preston never came back to claim them.

As a result, a certain protocol is followed: Preston was sent registered letters to claim his property. He never responded. After sixty days has elapsed, this personal property is considered surrendered and destroyed.

Gotcha.

I took possession of Preston's cell phones just days before they were going to be destroyed. Had I not claimed the phones, they would have been lost forever. After taking possession of these phones, I charged the batteries and checked the memory of the phones in an attempt to retrieve the phone numbers assigned to these phones.

I was hoping to get a list of associates or the phone book that Preston was calling during this time. I was also trying to determine if any Arizona numbers matched up to any of the guys we had already identified in this investigation—specifically if any phone numbers matched any known numbers we had for Richie Gomez. This research was successful to a certain extent, without getting a direct link to Gomez.

High-level drug dealers get several cell phones and discard the phones after using them for a short period of time. The practice of using multiple phones at any given time makes it difficult for law enforcement to track phone activity of an individual.

Another documented incident occurred when Gaylan was stopped for speeding on the highway about three weeks before the murders. During this stop, over a pound of marijuana was recovered from Gaylan.

The state trooper who did the traffic stop made photocopies of all the papers that were with Gaylan Green at the time. These included bank receipts and many credit cards. It was from this source of banking information that the financial research on our suspects began.

17
SHOW ME THE MONEY

Financial research is not really all that exciting. You don't get a big adrenaline rush from it. The only thing worse is looking at phone records. Unfortunately, both tasks have to be done, and sometimes records can produce really good evidence.

With Preston Blade and Gaylan Green, this research came in several ways. We received historical information on their real estate acquisitions and their vehicle purchases. This type of research is simple enough by contacting the county assessor's office for research on real estate, which generally gives either a previous and/or a current note holder.

After obtaining this information, we can serve subpoenas on these financial institutions to actually obtain contracts from the specific purchases. This same tactic is also employed with vehicle purchases by contacting the Department of Motor Vehicles.

So with this, in conjunction with the past information copied from previous arrests, we determined that at least five banks had business dealings with Preston and Gaylan within the last year. Subpoenas were sent to each bank, requesting all account history on Blade and Green.

The results of these subpoenas were intimidating to say the least. Just mountains of paperwork. After a while, you adjust yourself to the different formats and processes used by each bank. It was through this process that some very conservative money totals were calculated regarding the spending and distribution of money going on with Preston and Gaylan.

It was also during this research that a very interesting fact was discovered. On May 3, one and a half days before the bodies were discovered, Gaylan rented a U-Haul truck from a business in northwest Omaha. I thought maybe our victims either got whacked in the back of this truck or this U-Haul could have been used to dump the bodies.

So I contacted the U-Haul business and subpoenaed the information regarding the truck rental by Gaylan at the time of the murders. The information provided by the U-Haul company showed that the truck was rented for a couple of days and only had thirty-two miles driven on it.

I wanted to see this specific truck, even though nearly a year had passed, but maybe some forensic evidence could still be inside, maybe some blood was in the cracks of the floor.

As luck would have it, the truck had been sold to a private company that worked on railroad cars. I talked to the owner of this company and explained my interest in this truck they had bought from U-Haul. The company owner thought the whole thing was pretty cool, but explained his use for the truck caused it to be very greasy and grimy, with metal shavings all over it because of the work on the railroad cars.

I had done some research on the actual truck itself and, even though it was a long shot, I had learned the floor of the truck was metal planking, and there is a groove and a channel underneath the groove on each piece in the floor. I thought this area could possibly be a location where blood could have traveled and maybe been preserved.

This business owner, on his own dime, shipped the truck back to Omaha from Detroit and had it delivered to our impound lot. Upon its arrival, we did our best to be like the *CSI* television show with a crime lab tech named Sonny Buvano.

We dismantled the planking of this truck, exposing these channels. We used alternate light sources and tested the area with Luminol, which is a chemical mixture sprayed on a surface. If it has contact with blood, elements in the blood cause a reaction that makes the Luminol light up or glow in complete darkness.

Unfortunately, we could not find any blood or any other evidence of our crime.

I was always impressed by, and greatly appreciated, the effort that the railroad car business owner showed us. I wish all people we contacted were so helpful.

Another helpful piece to the puzzle came to light during the financial research. On March 16, Gaylan's credit card had a debit for $218 from the Hawthorne Suites, a hotel in Atlanta, Georgia. With that, we now completed verification, putting all our players in Atlanta to consummate the drug deal, as we had learned from statements from the Arizona crew.

Just to be thorough, I thought I would contact the Hawthorne Suites to obtain the actual receipts, check-in documents, or any other room service signatures associated with the room on Gaylan's credit card. Lady Luck, who had been on our side so far during this investigation, definitely took a break.

The Hawthorne Suites had been sold to Shepherd's Hospital as a long-term stay location for family members of long-term patients. However, while conversing with the assistant manager at the Shepherd's Hospital facility, he knew the old manager when it was the Hawthorne Suites.

I got in touch with the old manager and the new facility manager on a three-way telephone call. The old Hawthorne Suites manager directed the new Shepherd's Hospital manager to a storage room in the basement of the hotel, where he had placed a bunch of old records just prior to the closing of the Hawthorne Suites.

Sure enough, two bankers' boxes of records were located. I had them shipped to me so I could take the time to go through them, looking for the specific charge on Gaylan's credit card. It was a good try, but it turned out that they weren't those types of records.

We were checking everything. We were making our case airtight. It took off the table a defense attorney's strategy of ever claiming crappy police work.

18
IN THE GRASS BUSINESS
(BUT NOT A LAWN SERVICE)

One thing I learned over my career is that I have to rely on my contacts if I'm going to be successful. I need help.

To that end, a good cop must develop contacts in different fields and businesses to get information and to understand the information that has been developed. Some of these contacts may require a subpoena to provide the information and some may not. The subpoena is a powerful investigative tool that was used to the extreme on Preston Blade and Gaylan Green. By the end of this case, over a hundred subpoenas were served on different people and businesses.

Some of the first contacts I made were to our friendly local utilities, which included gas, electric, phone, and cable. I would also add that having contacts in specific businesses is much more efficient, so you don't just call a main telephone number and ask around, because you could actually end up talking to someone who knows your suspects, thus compromising the entire investigation and causing the bad guy to "turtle up" (not break the law) and make catching him impossible.

As a result of my utility contacts, I was surprised our targets had their names on several different properties. So the basic daily routine of surveillance began by checking out locations associated with Preston and Gaylan. At the peak of this investigation, Roscoe and I had fourteen locations we would either do stationary surveillance or drive-by surveillance, trying to determine the daily activities and routines related to Preston and Gaylan.

After serving an ex-parte order to the IRS, I obtained tax information on our suspects. The results were surprising. Preston and Gaylan either had little or no income for several years prior to the murders, but in their last tax return, which would have been the year following the murders, each had claimed income of $225,000 and each paid over $30,000 in federal income taxes, listing their professions as a lawn service and professional services.

A lawn service? Well, they were in the grass business, but it wasn't cutting lawns. Speaking of the lawn service, during our daily surveillances, we would see Preston driving a truck that had a lawn service decal on the doors: U-A-F Lawns. By observing this decal, I checked utilities for the business of U-A-F Lawns and located a commercial property that was rented by Preston and Gaylan for their lawn service.

During surveillance over an extended period of time at this location, we never saw a lawn mower, trimmer, blower, or anything remotely connected to yard work. However, there was a considerable amount of traffic that went in and out of the building through a large garage door that opened to allow vehicles to drive completely inside the building. During these surveillances, I always wondered what was inside. I knew it had to be criminal, but I'd have to wait for the day we could get inside to know exactly what was going down.

The actual property owners of this building were identified and researched. These people appeared to be legitimate business people so, as an investigator, I had to calculate the risks. Should the property owners be approached to get details, contracts, occupation dates of the property? This ultimately came down to a gut call.

The property owner was approached and served with a subpoena. This property owner cooperated fully, but was admonished of the penalties if he divulged any of the information regarding the subpoena to Preston or Gaylan. It was also learned from the conversations with the property owner that Preston and Gaylan had installed a high-speed, commercial-grade, garage door in the building that had cost thousands of dollars—

an interesting purchase for a lawn service that had no lawn equipment.

More importantly, this location was excluded as a possible murder scene because Preston and Gaylan took possession of it a few weeks after the murders.

Where had these murders taken place?

19
THE BARBER SHOP

As a result of the research on utilities, we found that Preston was paying for electricity at a commercial property—a bay in a small strip mall. This property was put on the surveillance list. As I drove by this property the first time and pulled up to it, I immediately recognized it as a barber shop that has come up on the narcotics radar before. As I watched this barber shop for a couple of weeks, it truly looked abandoned with no activity.

Another thought was running through my head based on the geographic location of this barber shop and the location where the bodies had been dumped so many months earlier. I thought, *If I had just whacked three people in that barber shop, where would I dump the bodies?*

In looking at the lay of the land of this barber shop, all directions would be poor except going in a northern direction, exactly where the bodies were found. I actually drove the route from the barber shop to the dump site, and it was less than three miles with only one turn, and the farther north I traveled away from the barber shop, the more sparse the land was with houses until it became wooded and very rural.

The location of the barber shop itself also was fairly favorable to concealing the sound of gunshots. The only other business in this small commercial strip mall was a laundromat that did not appear to be very busy or even open at night. The busy street would also produce some sound concealment because of traffic noise. The bay to the south of the barber shop was empty, and there were only a few houses up from the barber shop on an unpaved road.

I again contacted the utility company to confirm the status of the subscriber at this location because surveillance had not produced any activity while we were watching it. Guess what? Preston had stopped paying for utilities at the barber shop the month following the murders. It apparently was a misread by the first person who provided me the subscriber information indicating that it was actually an active account.

So, in analyzing this, the murders happened in early May and Preston was out of this property before the first of June.

We then began to research the people who actually owned the entire strip mall and the laundromat, and they appeared to be legitimate business people. With another gut decision, we decided to make contact with these people, feeling that it was not all that risky, to obtain as much historical information regarding the renting of the barber shop by Preston and Gaylan.

We also wanted to determine what the status of the bay was at this time and if the bay was vacant. We wanted to ask for permission to search it for any forensic evidence. Also, if there were new occupants, we wanted information on those people so we could research them.

Luck was back on our side. The barber shop bay was still empty and was only used as a storage location for the property owners. The property owners further described that the moving out by Preston and Gaylan was somewhat unusual.

The property owner said the rental agreement listed the business as a barber shop, titling Preston Blade as the president and Gaylan Green as the vice-president of their company. The property owner said Preston and Gaylan did not actually cut hair, but they had some barbers and stylists who did the work.

We also found out that only a short time before Preston and Gaylan moved out of the barber shop, Preston actually had asked about buying the entire building, but nothing ever evolved because the property was not for sale. Then, without notice or any complaints, Preston and Gaylan just moved out quickly.

Permission to search the barber shop was granted, so Roscoe Hogan and I, along with Crime Lab Tech Sonny Buvano, whom we had known our entire careers, prepared to search the bay.

Sonny had started his career as a jailer, but changed careers to become a crime lab technician. He was a logical thinker who was blue-collar and not afraid to work hard and get dirty. In one case, detectives were looking for evidence at a house where a woman had been poisoned with antifreeze, and Sonny had the right instinct to check the sink trap—and there was the physical evidence to put the perpetrator away.

We explained to Sonny that we thought this could be the actual murder location for the three bodies found burning several months earlier.

Based on the blood trails located at the original scene in the woods, it would be logical to think that a significant amount of blood would have been present at the location of the actual killings.

We developed a plan to do a covert, full-blown forensics search of this commercial property. We had to be covert because Preston and Gaylan were still free and driving all over Omaha, and this location was on a main thoroughfare and would easily be in their normal routes of travel. So parking a big police crime lab van in front of it could alert them that we were on to them.

In real police work, when the bad guy does not know if he is being watched, it makes things much easier. The bad guys continue their daily activities, actually gaining confidence and hopefully making mistakes.

We blacked out the bay windows with paper, dropped off equipment and workers, then drove away, and walked back to complete the search. We used alternate light sources and Luminol to complete this search. This is why the windows of the bay were completely blocked out. We needed a completely dark environment to check for any evidence of blood in the barber shop.

We searched every inch of the area, looking for anything, but no such luck, nothing was found. It was still a perfect place to do the killings.

20
DIGGING FOR DOPE

The research process was never ending. I wanted to establish the connection between Phoenix and Omaha with Preston Blade and Gaylan Green. To do this, I decided to subpoena the entire airline industry and vehicle rental records to establish a timeline that supported statements by Jesse Romo, Adam Romo, Kenny Boston, and Beto Rojas regarding Preston and Gaylan and their Arizona marijuana connection.

I cultivated contacts with every airline and, over an extended period of time, developed an extensive flight history. Preston and Gaylan were frequent flyers to and from Phoenix for a year before the homicides. This by itself means nothing, but as a piece of the puzzle in the entire case, it definitely is crucial and keeps the case going forward.

It was now time to get the U.S. Attorney's office involved and the County Attorney's office up to speed on how things were evolving. As with all things in life, you have your good and your bad. The same philosophy applies with prosecutors. This was going to be, or should I say, had the possibility to be one of the biggest cases in our department's history and would certainly be complex.

The right prosecutor would be essential for a positive end result. The prosecutor for this case would need to be highly motivated, organized, and have some instinctive ability to decide when to push the case forward and when to wait for details to evolve on their own. Luck was still on our side.

The U.S. Attorney assigned to this case was Lillian Lomax, whom I called Lilly. Lilly had all the needed skills. I had worked with her before, successfully, several times, both when she was a County Attorney and now as a U.S. Attorney. She possessed style and presence in the courtroom that was challenged by none in the federal district. Lilly was extremely smart with a certain edginess, so you did not want to piss her off.

Our actual plan was to first indict federally on drug charges and then, we hoped, the murder case would be developed, so we could follow that up with murder charges on the state side. On the state side, the County Attorney that would be assigned this case, if it was ever developed to that actual stage, was Georgeann Goldstein.

I had worked past murder trials with Georgeann, and she actually may be the smartest woman I have ever known, excluding my wife, of course. Her preparation for trial was intense and flawless. Georgeann was also one of my contacts whenever I had any legal questions. She would always provide me with the legal ramifications of a certain action that I was thinking of taking during an investigation.

Even though we had come a long way in this investigation, we still weren't anywhere near a murder arrest, and Lilly Lomax wanted some physical evidence before anyone got indicted. That meant we needed to get some dope.

21
LEGAL ROBBERY

As research was now in full gear, a piece of information surfaced from the narcotics unit. The narcotics lieutenant at the time remembered an airport interdiction stop of Preston Blade when he was carrying over $47,000 cash and was traveling to Arizona. This would have happened when Preston was most likely dealing with Kenny Boston or one of the other Arizona crew members.

The money was seized and Preston never made a claim for it, so it ended up getting forfeited to the city's general fund. As a result of that interdiction stop, Preston was assigned to be checked out by two narcotics investigators. I guess they did not find anything out because nothing ever came from that assignment. That was too bad because it was well before the murders ever happened.

During the interdiction stop, however, all items on Preston's person were photocopied by the airport authorities. This produced more banking receipts, which opened up additional avenues for research regarding financial records.

Ultimately, the research regarding the banking receipts of Preston and Gaylan took several months. These banking records showed large cash deposits and withdrawals in and out of several bank accounts. Often these transactions were over $10,000, but were never reported as suspicious by anyone in the banking community.

Banks are required to report suspicious banking activities and deposits over $10,000 in cash to authorities; however, this was never done at any time regarding Preston or Gaylan. Nonetheless, this information was documented and could be used someday in an affidavit or some type of legal paperwork during the progression of this case.

22
UNLIKELY ASSOCIATES

As I continued the phone number research, I knew it would likely lead somewhere in this case. It always does in dope cases. I believed a wiretap, which, legally is called a Title III investigation, would have to take place on Preston Blade's and Gaylan Green's phones.

First I thought we could get some marijuana deals on tape, but even more creatively, I thought we could push a few buttons and re-energize the murder case in the media in an attempt to catalyze conversation between Preston and Gaylan or others yet unknown, specifically about the murders. Before the court would authorize that level of intrusiveness, we had to exhaust all other investigative avenues or give reasons why other investigative techniques would not be successful.

So with a wiretap in mind, I tried to exhaust everything. During this process I subpoenaed phone records from the old cell phones taken from Preston when he was arrested at the hospital and never claimed and from phone numbers of Preston's that we obtained off the rental papers when he rented the lawn service business front. We had to wait for these records, which usually took several weeks or months. Even with contacts at the phone company, in reality, the cell phone companies are swamped with these types of requests and subpoenas. It just takes time.

Once we get these records, we analyze them for call frequency to see who the target is calling. Generally, it is the target's home phone number and his girlfriend that are at the top and then his co-conspirators in whatever crime he is involved in are somewhere next on the list. Sure enough, Preston and Gaylan talked like a couple of little girls.

One number, however, was very high on the frequency list, making it a telephone number of interest. A subscriber subpoena was completed on this number, which produced the name of Rick Ginney.

When we researched Rick Ginney, we found he was a fifty-five-year-old white guy with a fairly clean record, but he did have one prior drug conviction nearly twenty years earlier. This was not a typical associate that we would expect of Preston and Gaylan, who were looking like a couple of high-level, gang-associated dope dealers.

A further analysis of Rick's phone number showed that he would regularly travel from Phoenix to Omaha and back several times. This was verified by observing the cell towers that his cell phone would hit while it was in use, actually showing a travel pattern going back and forth between the two cities—Phoenix and Omaha.

As Roscoe and I developed this information, we debated about taking a shot at Rick Ginney, approaching him and seeing what he would say. This was risky because if he didn't say anything and reported back to Preston or Gaylan about our contact, we had nothing. We were not at a point to make any arrests in this investigation.

But on the other hand, if Rick Ginney cooperated, hell, he could have been a witness to the murders. Who knows? He may have even committed the murders. But we decided not to approach Rick yet. The risk was too high and the investigation was still going forward.

We added Rick Ginney to our associates chart. *Who is this guy?*

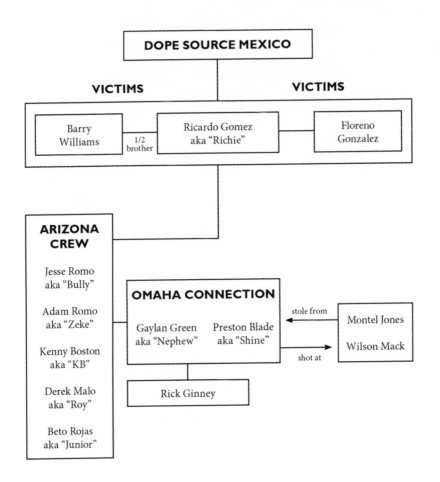

23
THE DEATH LOAD

As the historical research continued, volumes of data from banks, cell phone companies, airlines, vehicle purchases, and rental contracts started to overflow my desk and a shelf above my desk.

People skills are fine, but you have to stay organized or you'll get overrun. Every day I was getting mailings back from subpoenas, emails, and reports. The sheer volume of paper was overwhelming. The murder books alone numbered at least nine or ten, so far, and these were the thick three-ring binders that contained police reports.

As I was updating my to-do lists, an exciting telephone call came in. A border patrol agent in Texas called the homicide unit. He had received a statement from a guy they arrested coming across the border with a ton and a half shipment of marijuana. I need to stress what a good job this agent did because this statement could have just slipped through the cracks, never having any follow-up done or a phone call made to our jurisdiction.

This load driver, who was identified as Eli Martinez, told the border patrol agent how about a year earlier he had delivered a load, nearly the same size he had just been arrested with, into Omaha, where it was received by two big black guys. Eli explained that in the original plan, he was to receive payment for the marijuana from these guys and drive the money back to a specified location after it was received.

Martinez said there was some problem or mis-understanding, and the money was not ready, so he waited in Omaha for a day or so, until he was instructed by the Mexican suppliers to return to Mexico without the money.

Eli, the load driver, then told the border patrol agent after he left Omaha, he heard that payment was never made and people were actually killed over this nonpayment.

This information was vague, but did seem to fit our investigation. I wanted to speak to Eli Martinez in person in an attempt to get more specifics about his actions while in Omaha. I also wanted Eli to see photo line-ups containing our parties of interest, Shine and Nephew, to see if he could pick them out.

Arrangements were made for a trip to Texas so this interview could take place. I was hoping they had Waffle Houses there.

Some interesting things came about during our interview with Eli Martinez. First, he assumed that the victims of the murder were the black guys to whom he had delivered the marijuana. Second, Martinez indicated when he would drive loads of marijuana to various locations in the United States, he would generally rent a Budget or Ryder moving van in his own name, but also had several aliases that he used. This would be something that could be researched. Third, he gave a very distinctive description of the house and the surroundings of the house where the marijuana was actually delivered in Omaha.

Unfortunately, Eli Martinez could not pick Preston Blade or Gaylan Green out of a photo line-up that was presented to him. The only thing he could specifically remember is that they were two large black males, and they had other black guys with them who were doing the physical labor of moving the bales of marijuana. The two large black guys did not do any physical work themselves.

Eli described the delivery to a single-family house, one story, in a neighborhood that was close to a busy street. The driveway was on the right side of the house as you face it, with a carport, but the driveway was not paved or was in very rough condition, and there may have been a T-intersection at one end of the street.

These are actually quite a few identifiers that could eliminate certain houses where we had been doing surveillance or confirm that one of these houses did indeed closely match where the marijuana was delivered. I immediately checked this description against all locations we knew of for Preston and Gaylan, but none of them fit with the exact characteristics described.

As I attempted to verify Eli Martinez's statements regarding the rental of a Budget or Ryder truck for the load to Omaha, I thought that should be fairly simple, listing a subpoena that had Martinez's real name and four or five fictitious names that he could remember.

The results did produce numerous rentals by Martinez and some of the aliases, however, none of the rentals fit exactly to a time period before our murders. Although Martinez's statements appeared to be legitimate, I could not verify the actual truck being used to come to Omaha.

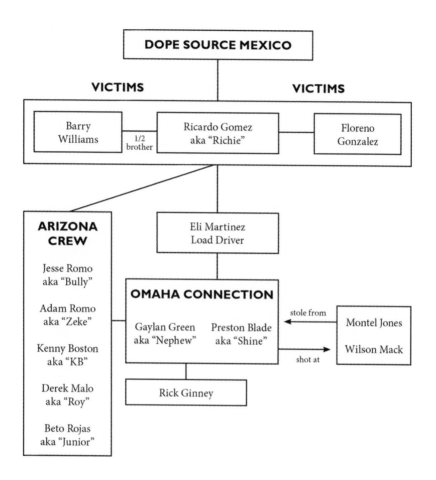

24
LOOKING
FOR THE STASH

As the research and surveillance continued, with the objective still being a wiretap on Preston Blade and Gaylan Green, information was developed on a new property just recently purchased by Preston. It was a single-family house, in a nice, quiet location in the northwest Keystone neighborhood of Omaha.

I would describe this location as a good area for a dope dealer who was carrying out his dope dealing activities on the near north side. This house was out of the hood, but close enough to get back to the hood quickly to attend to any issues in the dope dealing business, like shooting people who rip you off.

This house was observed to have numerous construction workers at it on a daily basis. It appeared it was in the process of being remodeled. Purchase agreements were subpoenaed from the title company, and we learned that Preston had put down $50,000 cash on the house.

It is not uncommon that dope dealers will use storage facilities to hide their drugs and cash. Up to this point, I had not even thought about that in this investigation. Whether that was from my heavy workload or the volumes of information coming in on this case or my own mere stupidity, but I did think of this possibility as I drove by Preston's new house one day.

Just a few blocks away from his new house was a big sign with an arrow pointing to Bernie's Mini-Storage and that's when the light went on in my apparently dark brain, *I wonder if they have any storage units.*

I drove right over to this secured storage facility and inquired with management about the renters. They wanted a subpoena, which I gladly obtained, and quickly located one unit in Preston Blade's name, one unit in Preston's girlfriend Yessica Tate's name, and one unit in Gaylan Green's brother's name, who was identified as Bronte Green. It should be noted that Bronte Green had surfaced in historical reports when Gaylan was shot and at the hospital. Bronte was arrested for disorderly conduct in the hospital emergency room that day.

Roscoe and I then began searching every storage facility in the Omaha area and located a total of nine storage units being rented by Preston Blade, Gaylan Green, and their girlfriends in two separate facilities, both in the northwest area of Omaha.

25
SURVEILLANCE
CLOSE CALLS

Life in this case became all about surveillance as we
continued to build our knowledge about the habits of
Preston Blade and Gaylan Green, the cars they were
driving, the associates they were meeting, and properties
they owned.

Speaking of known vehicles, I was amazed. We
had documented that Preston and Gaylan had several
vehicles: two brown, newer, matching Chevy Suburbans
and two newer, dark-colored, extended-cab pickup
trucks. There was a newer Chevy Monte Carlo that
they both drove, although it was registered in Gaylan's
girlfriend's name. Preston Blade had the white pickup

truck with the U-A-F lawn decals. Preston also had a newer, maroon Cadillac Escalade.

They each had matching, brand new Dodge Magnums, and Preston also had just purchased a one-year-old Chevy Corvette. These were vehicles that we had seen or documented from purchase agreements.

One day during surveillance, Roscoe and I were sitting in a narcotics undercover car, which was identical to the maroon Chevy Monte Carlo owned by Preston and Gaylan. We positioned ourselves in a car wash parking lot, just to the north of the lawn care business front. We were hunched down in a tinted window car. I thought it was a pretty good surveillance location.

After twenty minutes of watching, we saw Gaylan come out of the building through the high-speed commercial garage door. He looked over at our car. I was thinking there was no way he could have made us.

The next thing I know, Gaylan drove right toward us. Roscoe was in the driver's seat of our car and pulled out nonchalantly in an attempt to defuse the situation, however, Gaylan was most certainly following us. We made several turns just to confirm that he was following us. No doubt about it.

Just think about that for one second. We're the good guys and he's the bad guy and now he was chasing us. I was thinking we had come too far in this case just to get burned. By now, both Roscoe and I had our guns in hand, figuring this could end in a very bad way. After all, we think this guy's good for three murders already. We decided to pull into a gas station to see how it was going to end.

Gaylan pulled up right next to us, and Roscoe rolled down his window and yelled in a brash way, "Why you following us, man?"

Gaylan said, "I thought you was somebody else."

The best I could figure is he thought it was his Monte Carlo being driven by his girlfriend or one of his other homies and they were playing chicken with him. Whatever it was, I knew it was too close for comfort.

A similar event happened a week later. I was driving a different car, and I drove by Gaylan's primary residence, which is on a cul-de-sac in a high-end neighborhood in northwest Omaha. As I was leaving the area, I crossed paths with Gaylan coming home, and he did a U-turn, but I lost him quickly. Gaylan was acting paranoid, which in turn made me feel paranoid, so we stopped doing surveillance for a week after that incident.

To add to my paranoia, at about this same time, my wife and I were in bed, nearly asleep. As the phone rang, I answered it. These calls were usually work related when they came in late, so I was not excited to answer it at all, but I did.

The voice on the other end said in a black dude, homey, dialect, "We know where you live."

I responded, "What did you say and who the fuck are you?"

My wife immediately sat up, knowing this is not good. The phone went dead. I told her to get the kids out of the house as I retrieved my gun and looked out the window. I really thought the shit was on.

Then the phone rang again, It was my brother-in-law, Dusty, who lives in Iowa. He had a party at his house and came up with this idea to call my house fairly late. He felt terrible. He sensed in my voice things weren't funny on our side of the phone. Now it is a funny story, and I always hold it over his head, so I guess it was worth it.

This case needed to move on one way or another. My work and personal life were completely consumed by this investigation. Unfortunately, my children even knew a lot about the case, even the smallest of details. For example, one day we went out for dinner, and my kids noticed a street sign that said "Blade Road." One of my kids said, "Is that your bad guy's street, Dad?"

My goal was to start writing the Title III wiretap application. This was a very long, in-depth affidavit that, at the state level, is processed through the state attorney general's office and, at a federal level, goes through the U.S. Attorney's office in Washington, D.C. It often depends on various factors which venue is used, and it really did not matter to me.

We just needed to hear some dirty calls. And fast.

26
DEUCE'S DOWN

As we continued surveillance, a newer Chevy Suburban started appearing at most of the known locations. This Suburban was wrapped with a decal in bright blue colors that covered the entire vehicle and had the logo "Deuce's Down Music" on it.

This vehicle stood out—not the MO (method of operation) I would take if I were a dope dealer.

We verified by the license plate that it was one of the matching brown Suburbans we had previously observed. Let me tell you that following a brightly colored Suburban covered in a decal is a blessing.

Following or tailing a vehicle is not easy, especially since you are trying to prevent your presence from being detected. You have to stay way back. Generally, in this investigation, we would watch locations and document the activity and not do straight tailing. To conduct straight tailing properly, several follow cars should be used with the support of an airplane.

We did, however, follow this decaled, blue Chevy Suburban to a business that was previously a nursery in the south part of Omaha—the complete opposite side of town in relation to most of the activity we had discovered of Preston and Gaylan.

Preston and Gaylan had just purchased this property, putting $60,000 cash down. It was going to be used as a recording studio in the corporate name of Deuce's Down Music—so we added yet another location for surveillance.

This appeared to be another business front in an attempt to hide drug proceeds. I do think that rap music is the dream of most kids from the hood, and even if the dream is sincere, I think it is often funded with drug and blood money.

Roscoe and I also received a telephone call from our Phoenix gang investigators, Joshua Howard and Adam Morris, who advised they found a house recently purchased by Preston in Phoenix, with a purchase price of $340,000.

We received the legal documents on this purchase, which described how a $102,000 cash downpayment was paid by Preston, which would be held in an escrow account until the sale was final. This would not be for twenty-four months because of local laws regarding real estate speculators turning property over quickly, driving up the real estate prices.

During the interim, rent would be paid by Preston Blade, who was now occupying the house. Joshua and Adam also said there was a brand new Range Rover parked in the driveway licensed to Preston—a $60,000 vehicle completely paid in full.

27
WIRETAP?

I would not say I was paranoid, but I was getting close. Logically, calculating the quantities of marijuana that by now have been reported in the interviews with Carlos Willis, Kenny Boston, Montel Jones, Wilson Mack, Jesse Romo, Adam Romo, and Eli Martinez, in combination with the financial data we had accumulated, this was definitely a multi-million-dollar marijuana business taking place in Omaha.

Certainly surveillances were now extensive enough to establish a few things: Preston "Shine" Blade and Gaylan "Nephew" Green did not run a lawn service that would produce any revenue to support the lifestyle and purchases we knew about, and continued surveillance by itself would not likely lead to any arrests. We needed a wiretap.

Before I put pen to paper on the wiretap affidavit, an idea popped into my mind that would serve multiple purposes. I suggested to Sgt. Bogowski that we do some after-hours covert search warrants in the storage units and see what we find. He just stared at me and asked me to explain.

I described how we could, after the storage facilities were closed, gain access, hire a locksmith to pick the locks, search the units, find some evidence of the marijuana conspiracy, and continue on with the investigation based on what we find. If we found nothing, lock things back up, say that we attempted it in our wiretap affidavit, and then we could show that we tried search warrants and they were fruitless.

On the other hand, if we found evidence, whether that was money, guns, marijuana, records, or whatever, we act accordingly. If we had to take evidence, we could stage it to look like a burglary.

After digesting this for a few seconds, Sgt. Bogowski said, "Where do you come up with these ideas? Let's do it." All the while, Roscoe was sitting next to me, grinning from ear to ear.

After seeing that Sgt. Bogowski was receptive to this idea, I thought we should push the envelope a little farther. I said to him, "Not only should we do this wiretap, but we should do an implant in the lawn service business front."

An implant is actually an implanted microphone so we can listen to conversations inside the location.

This is, by far, one of the highest levels of intrusiveness that law enforcement can employ. To perform an implant-type of investigation, extensive surveillance must be conducted on the target location prior to the implant, in addition to devising a high-level security plan when the implant is put into place—we would have to actually break into the target location.

Perimeter officers would have instructions to intervene in some way with parties of interest if they returned to the area of the property prior to the exit of the team that was installing the implant. This could lead to some very nontraditional interaction between law enforcement and a suspect.

Sgt. Bogowski was a practical person, bringing me back to reality, stating, "Let's do one thing at a time. Let's concentrate on the search warrants first."

But in the back of my mind, I was thinking a wiretap and an implant would be the Mount Everest of investigations and that would be fun.

28
MAKING PAPER

By this time in my career, I had probably written between seven hundred fifty and a thousand search warrants. The process of writing a search warrant is actually the completion of two documents: the search warrant, which describes the place to be searched and items that are being sought during the search warrant, and the affidavit, which clearly documents the probable cause for the search warrant. This, in basic terms, tells the story of the investigation.

In a normal, routine narcotics-type search warrant, it takes a couple of pages to complete the affidavit. Nothing about this case was normal, so to fully describe the scope of the investigation, the affidavit I wrote was fourteen pages long.

Usually, when a judge signs a search warrant, the officer will take it to the judge, who will read it while the officer waits, and then sign it if the judge deems that probable cause does exist. This time, I left the affidavit and search warrants with the judge to read overnight because of the complexity of the affidavit.

After the warrants were signed for the nine storage units directly connected to Preston or Gaylan, we had ten days to execute the warrant. In this case, we had waited a year since the murders, so what was the rush?

We put together our raid team, which consisted of Sgt. Bogowski, Roscoe, Sam "Scrap Iron" Golic, and me. We got together and figured out which night in the next ten nights would work best for each of our schedules. That, in and of itself, was completely opposite of how the life of a homicide detective works. Generally, when the call came on a murder, you dropped everything and went to the scene or to whatever assignment you were given.

I can't tell you how many times I have left my wife at dinner or at a movie because of this process. I've missed family functions and hundreds of kids' sporting events. This job really was a burden. I had always heard of old timers who had worked in homicide for ten- or fifteen-year stints, and I could not figure out how they did it while juggling all of life's other responsibilities.

But now we were scheduling the most convenient time to do our covert, burglary-style, search warrant.

29
LEGAL BREAK(IN)

I made arrangements with the management of both storage unit facilities to have access codes for entry into the secured and gated lots after hours. Sgt. Bogowski, Roscoe, Scrap Iron, and I met around 11:30 that night in a parking lot near one of the storage units.

I arranged with a local locksmith to meet us at this location to assist in picking the padlocks on the doors. I was wondering how long it would take the locksmith to pick the locks because he was being paid by the hour, and I didn't want the bill to be too high, not to mention the great anticipation I had about what we would locate inside each of the units.

After everyone arrived, we doubled up in our vehicles, and the locksmith followed in his van to the first storage unit. I punched in the security code given to me by the storage facility personnel three separate times to get one vehicle in each time, because the gate closed quickly after a vehicle traveled through for security purposes. We were parked in front of the first unit Preston rented.

I tried to keep my expectations realistic. I truly hoped we would recover some articulate drug records or possibly some connection with our Arizona parties. I did not have any real anticipation that we would actually find any large quantities of marijuana because during the writing of these affidavits, one of the processes I used to gain probable cause was to have a narcotics dog sniff each of these units in an attempt to alert for the smell of a controlled substance. This, in and of itself, would have provided the probable cause for the search warrants, but the dog did not alert, which caused me to write the affidavits in detailed fashion, documenting the entire investigation.

As the locksmith began to pull out his tool bag, Sgt. Bogowski and I stood maybe twenty feet away from the unit as Scrap Iron and Roscoe stood directly next to the locksmith. I looked at my watch so the time could be documented in the reports as to when this process began.

After only about ten to fifteen seconds, Roscoe yelled over to Sgt. Bogowski and me, "He's got it."

My first thought was this is very cool because the bill for the locksmith's time wouldn't be too big. The garage-type door was pushed up.

Inside we saw a 1985 Cadillac El Dorado that had been backed into the storage unit. We decided to have the locksmith go to the next unit within the facility to open that lock so we could get him off the clock as quickly as possible.

Scrap Iron and Roscoe entered the unit and started searching it while I was jotting down a few notes on a notepad. Not more than a minute or two had passed when I heard Roscoe say, "Bo, you gotta see this."

Now I've been on the job long enough and at hundreds of warrants and I know the sound in someone's voice when they find something good. Something happens to their voice, whether it is excitement, happiness, or just out of being the man who found the shit, I don't know, but you sure know the sound in someone's voice when you hear it.

In the seconds it took me to get from outside the storage unit to the back wall where Scrap Iron and Roscoe were standing behind the Caddy, thoughts of grandeur were going through my head.

Could it be the wallets? The IDs of our murder victims kept as trophies? Maybe some marijuana? Even if it was marijuana, I figured the maximum amount that could be stored in the trunk of a car couldn't be more than 300 or 400 pounds, which would still be good.

As I got to the edge of the trunk and looked inside, I saw an 18-inch-square red cardboard box overflowing with money and a 3-foot-square safe directly next to it. Now I have seen large sums of cash in my career before, ranging from $10,000 to $250,000, but I quickly speculated that just the box, regardless of what was in the safe, was going to top that.

After a minute of high-fiving and acting very unprofessional, reality set back in. What should our next move be?

First, we needed to get crime lab to this location to photograph the storage unit as it was, photograph the opening of the safe when we opened it, transport the money and whatever evidence we found back to central station, and book in the money. We also still needed to get inside the other units within this facility, keep them secure until we searched them, and get the locksmith out of there.

Those were all jobs that needed to be performed just in the searching process, but what about in terms of how we played this in our investigation? If we took the money, which we would, and made it look like a burglary, my fear was Preston and Gaylan would be hunting for somebody to hold responsible, and I certainly did not want that to happen. We had a few hours to think about how we would play it as we processed this scene.

Once crime lab arrived and photos were taken of the first storage unit as it was, with the money and the safe in the trunk of the Cadillac, we then removed the safe and broke it open. And sure shittin', it was full of money. I mean literally jammed full of money. There was not room left for another Franklin, which was probably why the red box was in there for the overflow.

Roscoe and Scrap Iron processed this area with one crime lab technician, while I walked over to the other unit, which was being secured by Sgt. Bogowski after the locksmith had gotten it open.

I'm sure during this time by himself, he was processing this chain of events. Sgt. Bogowski was one top-notch homicide detective and sergeant, but this narcotics stuff was a little out his element. We talked about it as we searched the second unit. What did we find in this unit? Fifteen one-pound packages of marijuana in one-gallon Ziploc bags. Definitely not the motherload, but all in all, we were happy with the night's events.

This marijuana would be the first physical evidence of marijuana that would be used by Lilly Lomax in her federal prosecution. But still, how do we proceed? We had a responsibility for public safety, so if we staged this as a burglary, it definitely could put some innocent person in harm's way.

I made a new suggestion to Sgt. Bogowski, but as a result of this new suggestion, I was definitely taking the prior goal of wiretaps and implants off the table. I suggested that we hit them as hard as we could right then. I described to the sergeant that by using the search warrants for the storage units as a template and by adding our results from what we had already found, I could write search warrants on every location that we had identified being directly connected to Preston and Gaylan.

These locations would include Preston's main residence on Fortieth Avenue, Gaylan's house, the lawn service business front, the recording studio, an apartment that Yessica and Preston maintained in a small suburb to the south that was in Yessica's name under government housing that she paid $8 a month for, the house purchased by Preston that was being remodeled, in addition to the remaining six storage units that had not been completed on that night.

Sgt. Bogowski liked it and that became our plan.

30
MONEY, MONEY, MONEY

Once we arrived at central station, after completing the first wave of warrants, we went to the homicide unit's conference room that had acquired the nickname "The Bomb Room." To this day, I don't know where the nickname came from, nor does anyone else I've ever asked, but that's what it has always been called, so I can only assume that it goes way back.

Before the money could be received into our property unit, it must be counted, so Roscoe, Scrap Iron, and I started by counting $50,000 piles, which would fit into a large property envelope. We then switched the bags with one of the other officers, who then recounted it for accuracy. We did this until six in the morning, rarely getting the same count on any bag, always being about $20 off either way.

Before we start counting the money in "The Bomb Room."

Meanwhile, Sgt. Bogowski was trying to organize and clear through the chain of command the idea of hitting multiple warrants later in the morning. To pull this off, several search teams, SWAT teams, and other support from areas such as crime lab, property, and other jurisdictions would likely be needed depending on how well things came together.

When the first secretary arrived at central station that morning, I contacted her right away and began writing the next wave of warrants, but before they could be served, all the money had to be counted and booked into property.

The total recovered from the trunk of that Cadillac ended up being $358,000. This was hand counted by two officers then recounted by a property room employee before it was accepted. Shortly after this, the property room purchased a money counting machine in an effort to speed up this process.

If money is recovered during the daytime in large quantities, it is generally taken to a bank and the bank would count it for us. But after hours, we had to rely on this process. The money was eventually taken to a bank to verify our accuracy, and I believe our count was only $200 off from the original number of $358,000. In my opinion, that's really not all that bad for a couple of cops, especially after they had been up all night and were working straight on adrenaline.

One other thing happened that morning, as I was sitting at my desk collecting my thoughts prior to writing the next wave of warrants. The narcotics unit lieutenant at the time had gotten wind of our recovery during the nighttime hours. This would have been the same lieutenant who had assigned two detectives to investigate Preston Blade and Gaylan Green from the airport interdiction—the ones who turned up nothing.

This lieutenant sat down in Isadore Demann's chair directly next to mine and said, "Pretty good night. I think one of my officers should take this case over now. We've got better people to do the follow up."

My response was quick and, I guess, bordering on insubordination, "Why don't you run that brilliant idea by Sgt. Bogowski."

I think this lieutenant quickly realized how fucked up this suggestion was, and walked away. That is typical of politics in the police department. Somebody was always trying to benefit or capitalize on someone else's work.

31
NO KNOCK, NO KNOCK, ANYBODY HOME?

It was nearly eight in the morning by the time I had completed the next series of warrants, which included Preston Blade's main residence that he occupied with his girlfriend, Yessica Tate, and their two children, on Fortieth Avenue in the middle of "gangland."

I also had a search warrant for Gaylan Green's main residence in a middle-class suburb in northwest Omaha that he occupied with his girlfriend and several children. The remaining search warrants were for the lawn service business front, the recording studio, the new house of Preston's that was being remodeled, Yessica's apartment in the suburb to the south, and a new house I found that was purchased by Preston that I thought could possibly be used as a stash house in the eastern portion of town.

All these warrants, in addition to the six remaining warrants that had already been written at the storage facility, were to be served.

Strategy was discussed at some point during the early morning hours because, in a perfect world, we would execute all these warrants simultaneously, but to do that would be impossible just because of limitations on SWAT team personnel, which would be used first at the two main residences.

Our plan was to have four separate search teams for the first wave of warrants and have them set up surveillance on four of these locations. The SWAT teams would execute the warrants at Preston's and Gaylan's main homes first, then, after those locations were secured, the SWAT teams would reorganize and go to the next two search warrants, which would be the lawn business front and the recording studio.

The remaining search warrants followed as search teams became available. As in all police strategy plans, we could change it as need be, depending on developments. Usually something did develop, change, or at least go wrong, so we were always prepared to adapt.

The first two warrants were executed, which was initiated by a telephone call from me after the judge signed the warrants. The warrant itself does not need to be on location at the entry time of the search, but it does need to be there before the police leave the property described in the warrant. The search warrant itself must be presented to the occupants or left at the premises, so before this day was over, I would be at each search warrant location throughout the city.

The Fortieth Avenue house of Preston and Yessica was believed to be their primary residence based on the surveillance already completed during this investigation and the fact that Preston would be seen in the white U-A-F Lawns truck parked at this house nearly 70 percent of the time.

As luck would have it, about three minutes before the SWAT team approached, Preston left the house and drove away. Surveillance team officers did not follow, so we now had one of our targets on the move. The house was hit with Yessica and the two children inside. The search team took control of the property, so the SWAT team could reorganize and change locations to the lawn service shop to meet up with that search team.

As this went down, the other SWAT team hit Gaylan Green's residence. Gaylan was home and taken into custody without incident. He was transported to the police station and put in an interview room to sit and wait until all the warrants had been served.

This job of transporting an arrest down to police central station was one that I always thought sucked. When I was a uniform patrol officer and had to do this, it really was boring. You took this guy downtown, put him in a room, and then sat outside the room until the detectives got there. I used to hate it, so I actually felt bad for the officer who ended up with this assignment because he was going to sit there for a long, long time.

This process was critical, however, because Gaylan is now isolated with no access to communicate with the outside, unable to give warning to Preston or others to run, or to destroy or hide any evidence.

With that said, it was an amazing thing how word got around in the hood when police started taking action. It spread like wildfire that the police were hitting locations associated with Shine and Nephew.

Fairly quickly, I got a phone call that money and marijuana were found in Gaylan Green's residence. I didn't have any specifics on quantities yet, but this was good news.

As things were progressing, the preparation for the first SWAT team to hit their second location was under way. The surveillance team for the lawn service business front, that will become the search team, were waiting for the SWAT team to approach. As the SWAT team was approaching the building, surveillance officers saw Preston drive by this location, but were unable to catch up to him to take him into custody.

Entry was made into the building. Nobody was located inside, but now we know Preston was aware of our activities. My belief was he would most likely go on the run. Because of this knowledge, we then recruited additional officers from various units within the police department to set up surveillance on all the other search warrant locations. My fear was that Preston would go to these locations and attempt to recover additional monies or marijuana before he went on the run.

The search team for the lawn service business front was led by the two officers I had worked with in narcotics for nearly nine years: Brandon Sweet and Jimmy Quinn. Roscoe came to assist soon after the house on Fortieth Avenue was secured. This was a good feeling when you know that the search will be conducted thoroughly and the reports would be well documented. When you work in a place like narcotics with people that long, they are like family and you truly entrust your life to them regularly, so I knew they would do a good job on this search warrant.

Soon after Brandon and Jimmy got inside the lawn service business front, Brandon called me and said, "Bo, you ain't gonna believe this, but there are huge bags of marijuana in here. I've never seen so much and there's a shitload of cars parked inside here."

Gaylan's truck seized at the lawn service building.

The back end of Gaylan's truck showing huge bags of marijuana seized during the warrant search. In each of the black trash bags were twenty gallon-sized bags of marijuana. Unprocessed bales sealed with duct tape are shown in the back of the truck.

Marijuana processed from bales into gallon Ziplocs, which nicely hold one pound.

Well, to say the least, I was pumped, but processing this first wave of warrants was going to slow things down since evidence was being found at the locations. The second SWAT team that hit Gaylan's moved on and made entry into the recording studio, which was also secured. The search team for that location confiscated many pieces of high-dollar audio recording equipment, along with numerous pieces of evidence that were consistent with unwrapping bales of marijuana.

A bale of marijuana might weigh between twenty and thirty pounds. To repackage it, the dealers would rip off the multiple layers of plastic wrap or black plastic trash bags and the duct or shipping tape and weigh out 464 grams (that's a pound), which fits perfectly in a one-gallon Ziploc bag. So to find used tape, cut and wadded up plastic, with marijuana seeds and leaves, we knew we had found the spot where a load had been broken up for street sale.

We continued to recruit additional officers from other units so other locations could be watched and the search warrants could be executed. Before the execution of the warrants at the storage facility, surveillance officers saw Preston drive by the intersection, directly in front of the entry into this storage lot.

The plain-clothes officers quickly began to follow as a uniform patrol car was called. Lights and sirens. Preston was taken into custody without any problems. Unfortunately, for another poor officer, the job of babysitting Preston now began until the end of the search warrant sweep.

The search teams then went back to the storage facility and began to execute the warrants there. These warrants were also productive. Jimmy Quinn and Brandon Sweet split up at this point, with Brandon remaining at the lawn service business front and Jimmy taking on activities as the lead officer at the storage unit because it appeared another large stash of cash was located, along with several hundred pounds of marijuana.

This huge task of securing, searching, and processing each location, using detectives borrowed from all units within the detective bureau of the police department, resulted in fourteen search warrants being served in relation to Preston and Gaylan on this day.

32
HAUL 'EM TO JAIL

After thirty-six hours of work, I was trying to get all the initial reports from each team. These consisted of a Receipt and Inventory Report and a Property Report, listing all the items of evidence that were removed from each specific location. It was at this point I could finally know exactly what had been confiscated during this investigative assault on Preston Blade and Gaylan Green.

Both guys were now sitting in separate interview rooms at the police department. Before each man was booked into jail on the appropriate charges, he was presented with a copy of the Receipt and Inventory Report, highlighting all the items that were taken.

These items included the following:

Bernie's Mini-Storage Unit 427: Thirteen one-pound packages of marijuana.

Bernie's Mini-Storage Unit 245: 1973 restored Chevy Impala.

Bernie's Mini-Storage Unit 246: 1985 Cadillac El Dorado with $358,000 cash.

Crown Storage Unit 135: $164,880 cash and a JVC 56-inch big screen television still in the box.

Crown Storage Unit 292: 1973 Chevy Caprice convertible.

Crown Storage Unit 478: Two bales of marijuana (total weight of 36 pounds), one KKSBR Model JI5 223 Assault Rifle with two boxes of ammunition.

Crown Storage Unit 350: 1984 Dodge Ram van containing 30 bales of marijuana (total weight of 716 pounds).

Lawn Service Business Front: 258 pounds of marijuana, a money counting machine, $81,970 cash found inside the pop machine, 2003 blue Chevy Suburban with complete body decal, 2004 blue Chevy truck, 2005 silver Dodge Magnum, 2005 black Dodge Magnum, 2004 Chevy Corvette, 2006 blue BMW 750 series with 250 miles on it, 2006 black BMW 750 series with 200 miles on it.

Gaylan Green's main residence: $22,990 in cash, 60 grams of marijuana, brown Chevy Suburban.

Yessica's Section 8 apartment: Numerous car titles, bulletproof vest, Arizona ID cards for Preston Blade, one camcorder, two cameras.

Recording Studio: Scales, shrink wrap with large quantities of marijuana residue, numerous pieces of recording studio equipment.

Preston's and Yessica's main residence: 189 grams of marijuana, digital scale, black Dodge Durango.

Money found inside the pop machine at the lawn service.

One of two matching BMWs seized inside the lawn service
building. Just to the left is one of their new Corvettes.

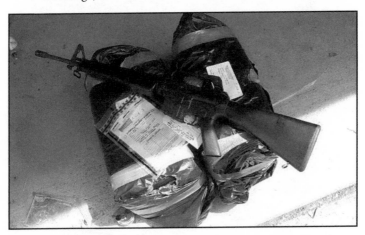

Two bales of marijuana and an assault rifle seized in a search of
one of the eight storage units.

Marijuana bales found inside an old van sitting at a storage unit
(total weight of the marijuana was 716 pounds;
street value $716,000).

It was now time to have my first real interaction with Preston and Gaylan—guys I had been tracking for months. I knew so much about them. I suspected they had murdered and burned the three Mexican men.

I want them to know I'm working homicide, not narcotics. I want them to start worrying. Maybe one would want to talk. That was my hope. But I didn't think it was realistic.

During this contact I also hoped to let them know the seriousness of what had happened over the last thirty-six hours and to let each of them know I was willing to listen to any statements they had to make.

The goal of this strategy was significant at many levels. Even if either one of them wanted to talk and gave me a lie or bullshit statement, that was okay, because I could attempt to disprove that statement, discrediting them later in court. However, the best scenario would be to have one of them roll over on the other, giving up the murders. This was not likely, but it does happen, so it had to be presented to them that they had an opportunity to cooperate.

Gaylan was first. If someone was going to talk, I thought it would be Gaylan.

I walked into a fourth-floor interview room of the Criminal Investigation Bureau at downtown police headquarters. Gaylan was sitting at the same table where he'd been sitting for nine hours while we were searching his house, the recording studio, the lawn service, the remaining storage units, and his secondary houses.

His head was down, he looked up at me and said, "What's up, man?"

He's a big guy, twenty-four years old, and tired from sitting in a ten-by-ten room all day. He wasn't handcuffed, but there was a guard outside the door.

"You got big problems," I opened the conversation. "I got a receipt and inventory of all the stuff we recovered today, and it doesn't look good." I handed him a list of the property seized.

"I'm a homicide cop, and that's what this is all about, so you might be in your best position right now to tell me what you know," I said. "If someone else wants to talk first, they'll get all the good things that come with it." And he chose not to talk.

I gave the same spiel to Preston. He had the same attitude. He wasn't talking.

Roscoe and I then walked Gaylan to the jail elevator and rode it to the basement of the police station. We put our guns in the gun locker and walked him into jail. He's booked in for his marijuana charges and taken to his concrete ten-by-ten cell in solitary confinement, which on the street has earned the name "Bedrock."

We did the same procedure with Preston.

A couple nights here should help build up the anxiety. My goal in these initial conversations was to get their anxiety up. Both Preston and Gaylan were booked on drug charges in state court with the plan of having a federal indictment in the near future; however, even though we had recovered a large amount of marijuana, in addition to the statements of Kenny Boston and Jesse and Adam Romo from Arizona, the overall weight of marijuana was not that significant in the federal sentencing guidelines.

The fallout from these warrants drew large amounts of media coverage, which produced several things that worked out to law enforcement's advantage. First, the report number I used for the search warrants was the same report number for the original murders. This caused the media to link the two events—again raising the level of anxiety for Preston and Gaylan.

I also contacted the Arizona gang officers, Joshua Howard and Adam Morris, with our results, so they in turn wrote a search warrant on the house purchased by Preston in their jurisdiction. As a result of this search warrant, a handgun and a paid-off 2006 Land Rover in Preston's name was located.

Because of the large amount of media coverage, a gentleman who owned a car restoration business called the homicide unit and told us that Preston and Gaylan currently had two vehicles at his shop that were having work done. One was a 1966 Chevy Impala and the other was a 1972 Monte Carlo. Both these vehicles were seized.

A few days later, Gaylan's girlfriend showed up at one of the storage units trying to recover some personal items such as toys and clothes that were not seized, which was fine with me, but she arrived with several other women in the maroon 2003 Monte Carlo that was the look-alike for our undercover car. I called uniform patrol officers to go to the storage unit and impound that vehicle.

The reason for this was twofold. First, this car was a forfeitable item because it was used during the conspiracy. Second, I wanted to send a message to Preston and Gaylan that we were still coming and we were everywhere, just trying to build that anxiety level, hopefully getting one of them to talk.

33
BLUE TRUCK?
BLACK TRUCK?
YOU'RE OUTTA LUCK

Over the next week I was still trying to process and organize the events from the search warrants. As this continued, it seemed as if the event had to be briefed and represented continually to different people.

It's kind of funny how in law enforcement when something good happens, people show up from other units and other agencies trying to get a piece of the action. With all the cars and money subject to be forfeited, this case was prime pickings for other crews and agencies to get money or cars for undercover work or their unit's use.

During one of these briefings we were talking about the vehicles, and during the discussion, Gaylan Green's

2004 blue truck was mentioned. I spoke up to correct the statement, saying that Gaylan's truck was black, and I had pictures of it from when he was shot and four pounds of marijuana were found in the back end at the hospital search.

With this discrepancy, I decided to go out to the impound lot where the vehicle was being held to check the VIN number and the color to determine if they were actually the same vehicle or if someone had misrepresented the color. After Roscoe and I located the vehicle at the impound lot, we confirmed the color was definitely a dark blue.

As Roscoe entered the vehicle to get the paperwork on the truck, Roscoe hit the console exposing a concealed compartment which had $16,000 cash, a .38-caliber handgun, and a scale. The luck thing was still happening. It turned out the VIN number on this blue truck was the same as the black truck. They were one and the same.

We later found out from the owner of the same car restoration auto body shop that, in addition to the two vehicles he had for Preston and Gaylan, he had also done previous work for Gaylan.

He described a paint job to a black Z71 pickup truck. It was painted dark blue, and the body style was changed to an SS-style. He also told us the existing bed liner was removed and a three-quarter-inch-thick bed liner was sprayed into it.

This extensive work—to a truck that was barely a year old at the time—cost nearly $8,000. The work was reportedly done in June 2005, just one month after the murders. We asked if the old bed liner was still possibly at the business, but our luck was not that good. I can only imagine how much DNA evidence was in that bed liner, wherever it was now.

This was interesting information and seemed to correlate with the information regarding the black truck at the intersection of Sixtieth and State the morning the bodies were located. We did conduct a complete forensic processing of this now-blue truck with negative results, which was not surprising because of the extensive work that was done on it.

It sure seems reasonable that this truck was used to transport the bodies that morning in May, nearly a year earlier. But we couldn't prove it.

Another interesting development. We were discussing some of the property that had been recovered, specifically, the two brand new BMWs located in the lawn service business front. These Beemers were paid off, in full, with no liens. Preston and Gaylan purchased them through an auto broker, providing cash to the broker, who then wrote business checks to the automobile dealer out of his own account. These two high-end BMWs had cost over $80,000 apiece.

During these initial meetings, top command from the police department, along with command from the FBI, were trying to put their dibs on these babies. In the end, rational thinking took over and these two luxury cars, along with several others, were sold at auction and the proceeds from this sale were put into an escrow account pending the outcome of the case. For this to happen, both Preston's and Gaylan's attorneys had to get both of them to agree to this arrangement.

After auction, nearly $300,000 was put into an escrow account based on the sale of the seized vehicles.

34
BAD MAN'S WOMAN

The day the warrants were served, I had brief contact with Preston's girlfriend and mother of one of his children. Yessica Tate went by the nickname "Yessy." She was a twenty-nine-year-old mother of two children, attractive, with no job and appeared to live off the proceeds of Preston's "business" or whatever type of public assistance she could get.

This contact happened when I was at the Fortieth Avenue house to provide a copy of the search warrant. This location was in the heart of the 40th Avenue Crip territory, a gang in which Preston was a documented member.

At times over my career, the 40th Avenue Crips were considered one of the most dangerous gangs known for shooting and killing rival gang members. The street corner of Fortieth Avenue and Pinkney Streets was, at one time just a few years earlier, one of the busiest crack cocaine selling corners in Omaha, which is just one block down the hill from the well-kept white bungalow with burgundy trim on the front now maintained by Preston and Yessica.

As much as Preston loved being in the hood and close to the action, I'm sure he definitely sensed the danger also associated with this location. I based this on his maintaining the apartment with Yessica in the southern suburb and his new purchase of the house in northwest Omaha.

As I presented Yessica with a copy of the warrant, she definitely played the victim role with me, crying and claiming she knew nothing. Yessica was also upset because the vehicle she drove, a black Dodge Durango purchased by Preston, was seized.

During this contact with Yessica, I asked her where she was going to be staying because this location would not be safe anymore now that Preston was in jail. The saying about honor among thieves really is true. I truly believed that if any thug out there thought Yessica knew where any more drugs or money were or if we missed anything, they would be at this house as soon as we left.

Yessica was not worried. She said she would be looked after by the neighbor across the street, which was where she was with her children when I arrived to deliver the search warrant. This trusted neighbor was a forty-three-year-old black man named Johnny Baustau, who spoke with a Southern drawl and worked odd jobs, with no regular employment. At the conclusion of this search warrant, Yessica was left at Johnny's house with my business card.

Within a day or two, Yessica called my cell phone and asked for some personal items of children's toys and clothing that had been left in the black Dodge Durango. As an act of good faith, I have always believed that doing good deeds, like providing these items to Yessica, was morally right. It was also good to document just in case some low-life defense lawyer tried to discredit me, then I could use these good deeds as a rebuttal.

Yessica got a personal delivery of car seats, toys, and children's clothing that were in the Durango.

Things had finally slowed down enough that right after we dropped these things off with Yessica, Roscoe and I decided to take a run at Rick Ginney, whose phone number was all over Preston's phone tolls, going back and forth between Phoenix and Omaha.

The media were still blowing up over the warrants and speculating on the connection to the murders. It would be the perfect time to approach Rick and get a statement.

As we pulled up in front of Rick's house, in an older part of southeast Omaha, where the houses had seen better days and most yards had junked cars rusting away in them, here was a white guy, fifty-five years old, with thick bushy hair that was six months past due for a cut and bushy mustache to match, working under the hood of a pickup truck.

As we got out of the car, we called to him, "Rick Ginney."

He responded, "Yeah, who's asking?"

We identified ourselves and our connection to the investigation on Preston Blade and Gaylan Green. We described to Rick how information was just starting to unfold, and we believed he may have some valuable information.

Rick was obviously nervous, as his voice was cracking and his hands were shaking. Rick asked if we were taking him to jail right now, which is generally a question spoken only by a guilty man. We explained to Rick that his knowledge meant more to us than putting his ass in jail and this was his opportunity to come clean. Even if he wanted to talk right then, I don't think he could have with his mind racing so quick and his voice trembling.

The situation was this: we weren't ready to arrest him, but it sure felt like he was going to be a piece to our puzzle. Ultimately, we left a business card with Rick and told him to call when he was ready to talk. We reminded him that the warrants were just the beginning, and he needed to decide whether he wanted to end up in front of the investigation or under the investigation.

By late April, just sixteen days after the original warrants, Preston and Gaylan were federally indicted, with an initial appearance in federal court set for May 1 and a detention hearing regarding their detention status to follow.

35
LOOKING FOR A DEAL

The proffer interview is a tool generally used in federal prosecutions, often in narcotics cases. The proffer interview gives the defendant an opportunity to cooperate with the government; however, none of the statements can be used against the defendant giving the interview, unless the statements are proved to be false. In return, the defendant in the federal system will receive consideration, which could reduce a pending sentence up to 50 percent.

This "let's make a deal" tool is crucial to law enforcement in conspiracy cases because the lower-level participants in a criminal conspiracy can give statements regarding the overall conspiracy. Law enforcement can then independently look for evidence to corroborate these statements with the goal of taking out the entire criminal conspiracy with conspirators at the top of the hierarchy getting the harshest penalties.

With all that said, and looking at our position in the murder case, we were not really at all close to solving the murder. So, with the May first initial appearance and detention hearings for Preston and Gaylan coming up soon, we were contacted by Preston's attorney, stating he wanted to proffer.

Well, this was interesting to say the least. We believed Preston to be at the top of our conspiracy, so this went against the normal idea of working toward the top guy if we talked to him. But we may have been dead in the water if we didn't talk to him. So a decision was made between Lilly Lomax and Georgeann Goldstein that a proffer interview was to be set up with Preston in the basement of the federal courthouse after his initial appearance and detention hearing.

The hearings took place with both Preston and Gaylan ordered detained by the federal court. Preston was then discreetly escorted by the U.S. Marshals to a basement interview room in the federal courthouse, unbeknownst to Gaylan or his attorney. Present in this interview room was Preston and Preston's court-appointed attorney, along with a second attorney, who also indicated she was representing Preston.

This co-representation was highly unusual because the court was paying the first attorney to represent him, so I wondered who was paying the second attorney, who identified herself as Rolinda Dupree. If Preston could afford to have an attorney on his own, I wondered why should the government and taxpayers (who I am one of) be paying for the court-appointed lawyer.

I'm sure the court took a conservative position, allowing both attorneys though, so if Dupree did an inferior job defending Preston by herself, then Preston could not, at a later time, make some type of claim or an appeal of inadequate counsel down the road.

I had not seen much of Rolinda Dupree in district, state, or federal court. I quickly inquired with Lilly what she knew about Rolinda Dupree. Lilly told me, "I'm not sure about her legal qualifications, but I have taken an exercise class with her before."

That little piece of history didn't help out any anxiety I was having. During the initial introductions and initial stages of this interview, it appeared that Rolinda Dupree was going to let the court-appointed lawyer take the lead at this point in the investigation.

After the procedural explanations were completed for the proffer interview to begin, Roscoe and I spoke with Preston.

I opened with, "Tell me about how the dope thing all started."

Preston didn't hesitate at all, much to my surprise. He then explained his evolution in the marijuana drug trade. He specifically named Kenny Boston and other members of the Arizona crew, describing how he would obtain loads of marijuana in Phoenix and then have them brought back to Omaha.

"It wasn't hard for me to figure out that Richie was the source of all the marijuana, so when we were in Atlanta I talked to him about getting my own big load brought to Omaha," Preston admitted.

"Rick Ginney," he said, "was my man. He was the one who drove all the loads back from Phoenix. The big load arrived in Omaha, and I gave Gaylan $335,000 cash for my half of payment. The day after I gave it to him, Gaylan gave me my money back and told me we could keep it, and the weed was ours too."

I asked, "Doesn't that give you a little suspicion because that's the same time the three dead guys were found, one of which is Richie, and you're not thinking based on what you just said that Gaylan didn't kill them? And that would be the first question I would have asked Gaylan. So did you ask Gaylan if he killed Richie?"

Preston replied, "I have trouble speaking with law enforcement because it goes against my nature."

Preston's court-appointed lawyer, who was sitting directly next to him during this interview process, appeared to have a look of shock on his face and interrupted, "Whoa, we're not talking about this stuff anymore."

The value of this interview, even though it would likely never be used in court, was huge. It confirmed several known facts.

First, we knew that Rick Ginney, the load driver, was a party of interest in this investigation, but now we definitely knew to go after him; and second, at some point in this investigation, Gaylan would find out that his partner, Preston, approached us and was trying to put responsibility of the murders on him. This should definitely push these two apart. Third, this was also confirmation of the Atlanta trip described by the Arizona crew.

36
EVASIVE
HOME INVASION

I hate it when I'm right. Two days after Preston's proffer interview, I was at home getting ready for bed when the phone rang. Nighttime phone calls never had anything good coming out of them.

This call was the same. A uniform patrol officer was calling. He told me he was at an address on Fortieth Avenue belonging to Yessica Tate, because of a home invasion robbery. I could hear crying and screaming in the background. I sensed a traumatic situation still unfolding. The officer indicated that the victim wanted him to contact me at home to advise me of the situation.

I did not talk to Yessica at this time because it appeared she was still hysterical, and I thought I would let the officers handle it. Yessica said she arrived home at about 9:45, and as she was entering the house with her two children, she was approached from behind by two masked gunmen who forced her into the house with the kids. Once inside the house, Yessica and the children were locked inside a closet while the gunmen ransacked the house.

Yessica said that no actual physical harm had happened to her and nothing was missing from the house.

I was skeptical of both of these statements. I would certainly not be surprised if Yessica was sexually assaulted; first, just because that's the kind of assholes that are out there, but second and more likely, they were sending a message to Preston that he didn't have any steam left on the streets. Nobody would ever know for sure because Yessica did not report it if it did happen.

As for no items of value being taken, I wasn't convinced of that either. The masked gunmen did not do this on a hunch. They must have had some reason to believe something of value was inside the house at that time, whether it was money or dope. It was also interesting to find out that Yessica was driving a new Buick Rendezvous that was registered in her grandmother's name.

We knew when the cops left that house on the fourth of April during the search warrants just a month earlier, the house was clean. Although, when cops do search warrants, they do miss items—remember that $16,000 cash and gun we found later in the center console of Gaylan's truck at the impound lot?

But why would the masked gunmen wait a month to rob the house? If they thought there was something left after the search warrants, they would have hit it right away. Just another question bouncing off the walls inside my very roomy head.

37
PILING ON THE CHARGES

Now that things had settled down a bit by mid-May, Assistant U.S. Attorney Lillian Lomax was on her game.

Based on all the evidence we had developed from the search warrants, follow-up interviews, and investigation, Lilly filed a superseding indictment on Preston Blade and Gaylan Green, which actually just meant adding additional charges or items to the original indictment.

On this indictment, not only was the original marijuana included, but also the firearms that were recovered, specifically, the handgun in Gaylan's truck, the rifle in one of the storage units, and the second handgun located during the search in Arizona.

Preston was a convicted felon, which actually added an additional charge for being a felon in possession of a firearm. Most impressively, on this indictment was an itemized list of property to be indicted, which included $710,388 of U.S. currency, nineteen vehicles, $37,351.82 in bank investment and escrow accounts, which were frozen, three parcels of real estate, miscellaneous musical recording equipment, including computers, keyboards, speakers, and microphones recovered from the recording studio, two big-screen televisions, a $4,000 gift certificate to a travel agency purchased by Gaylan, and all jewelry, including three watches located in Preston and Yessica's apartment. The watches and jewelry were appraised at over $30,000.

This indictment was impressive to say the least, but the greatest value was that it started the prosecution clock all over. What this meant was that after an indicted person had his initial appearance in federal court, the judge started the clock with the goal of being to trial in seventy days. There are many ways to stop this clock based on motions to suppress by either the defense or prosecution. In essence this rule kept the wheels going and the justice system moving, but for our purposes, since this case was still unfolding, this started the seventy-day clock over, which gave us more time to go after more co-conspirators and start listening to their phone calls and trace phone records.

38
THE DOPE DRIVER

Preston's proffer interview, which I believe contained strands of truth in it, specifically identified the relationship with Rick Ginney as his load driver. My interaction with Ginney could be valuable in this case. He could be the key to getting the most accurate and the highest amount of marijuana to actually be associated with this conspiracy.

Accounting for quantities of marijuana can be difficult. When talking to each member of a conspiracy, for example, the guys in the Arizona crew, each of those members can only say what they did themselves. It was apparent that Preston and Gaylan were working each of those individuals against each other at some point.

Rick Ginney was the common denominator. He could shed the most light on the number of trips and the quantities of marijuana.

If the weight reached higher levels, the penalties in federal court would dramatically increase. So now, with Preston's proffer statement, I could go back at Ginney, who gave his first statement in which he minimized his involvement dramatically. I don't blame him for trying, but now that I developed the answers to my questions before I asked them, it was not a good plan to try and play me.

As an investigator, I analyzed my situation. My position had definitely changed since the search warrants. My original goal of wiretap and possible implant was obviously out the window with the raids and the arrests of Preston and Gaylan. My goals now had to be raising the level of marijuana so the penalties were increased and wrapping up as many co-conspirators in the deal as possible, with the hope that somebody would talk about the murders so they could be solved.

Before we got our next crack at Rick Ginney, the real world of police work struck. I had to get ready for a trial on an old murder case. That not only meant preparing myself, but meeting with the prosecutor and tracking down witnesses and bringing them to the prosecutor's office for reviews of their statements. The entire process was painstakingly slow and meticulous. However, if these steps were not taken, success was not likely in the courtroom, so Roscoe and I put this case on hold for the next four weeks.

After the trial, Roscoe and I called Rick Ginney and told him we needed to talk to him further about his statements. He was receptive and an appointment was set up for June 6.

Rick arrived at the police station and was taken to an interview room, which was equipped with both audio and video recording equipment. Rick was advised he was not under arrest and was free to leave at any time. We only wanted him to be completely truthful with his statements. This was an important statement because Rick was not Mirandized at the beginning of this contact with him. Miranda rights apply only to people who are in custody, and Rick was free as a bird at this time.

"I just want to tell you," he said immediately, "I had nothing to do with the murders, but I'm worried about the drug end of this thing."

"It's your choice. If you want to talk," I told him.

And talk he did. He began to talk for several hours, describing how he came to meet Preston. Rick described how in the late 1980s he was working at a gas station at Fortieth and Bedford Streets, which was in the heart of 40th Avenue Crip territory.

Rick said he met a neighborhood guy named Chuck Nissan, and it was Chuck who quickly introduced Rick to crack cocaine. Rick soon became addicted to crack cocaine, using it for the next ten years of his life. During this time, Rick said Chuck Nissan caught a crack cocaine case and went to prison for a while.

"After Chuck got out of prison, we started hanging out again," Rick said.

"When?" I asked.

"Around Christmas time in 2004 or right after," he said, "and we went to Denver to meet up with an old prison contact to get a hook-up on weed to turn a quick buck. But we couldn't find the guy, so we kept on driving down to Phoenix."

"And?" I prompted him.

"Hell, yah. Bout three pounds. No problem. We met a dealer in a gas station parking lot," he boasted.

Isn't that ironic? This is the same way Preston Blade and Kenny Boston originally met. I think Phoenix gas stations should have signs on their marquees that say, "Marijuana hook-ups available here."

Two weeks later, Rick said, they made another trip to Arizona and got eleven pounds of marijuana from a different source, but it was also very easy. After returning to the Midwest, Chuck told Rick he may have a new deal for them.

Rick told us Chuck explained that he had a guy who wanted them to drive loads of marijuana from Phoenix to Omaha. This guy's name was Preston "Shine" Blade. It all made sense. Chuck Nissan was from the Fortieth Avenue hood and so was Preston Blade. Rick Ginney worked at the gas station there where he had met Chuck years ago.

Rick said they all met in the parking lot of a casino in Council Bluffs, Iowa. At this time, Preston provided Chuck and Rick $500 cash upfront for gas and expenses. They then drove to Phoenix in Rick's Silverado pickup, checked into a Motel 6, and waited for Preston to call them.

Preston called within a day and met Chuck and Rick at the motel in possession of 150 pounds of marijuana, which Rick and Chuck drove back to Omaha. Rick said Chuck slept the whole way back, leaving him to do all the driving.

Once back in Omaha, Preston gave Rick and Chuck eight pounds of marijuana to split as payment for their driving services. Rick said he and Chuck did two more of the same deals within a month: one for 200 pounds and one for 400 pounds.

The marijuana is packaged in bales weighing twenty to thirty pounds each. Bales would be about eighteen by eighteen inches by two feet (about twice the size of a computer tower). They would fit nicely in the bed of a pickup enclosed with a tonneau cover.

Rick then described how Chuck got greedy and wanted to raise the price on Preston. Rick explained as Chuck was trying to raise the rate of pay on Preston, he was standing behind Chuck and was trying to make eye contact with Shine trying to convey that he was not going along with Chuck's idea at all. Rick said nothing came from this interaction, but it appeared that Preston was pissed off.

Rick said shortly thereafter Preston called him directly and the two of them negotiated a new deal in which Rick would be the only driver. It was decided he would receive six pounds of marijuana and $1,000 cash for each load he brought back to Omaha, regardless of how big the load was, leaving Chuck Nissan completely out of it.

Rick loved this new proposal because he described how Chuck wasn't doing any of the driving anyway, so now he was getting more payment for the same amount of work.

Over the next six months Rick did at least twenty runs, averaging at least 500 pounds per load. He described how he kept an oil change chart so he could estimate the number of trips off this chart. Rick also said he generally checked into the same Motel 6 under his real name, so there should be some record of his stays in Arizona. This was also nice because it gave Roscoe and me another reason to travel to Arizona. Waffle House, here we come.

Rick was putting so many miles on his pickup truck that he bought a second truck specifically for marijuana runs and had to put a tonneau cover over the bed of this truck because the loads were so large.

At some point during this "business" relationship, Preston got stopped at the airport with a large amount of money. This would have been the interdiction stop the narcotics officers tried to follow up on Preston long before the murders. From that point on, Rick was entrusted to drive the money down to Arizona. Then Preston would take possession of the money in Arizona, obtain the marijuana, and bring it back to the motel for Rick to bring back to Omaha. That's a lot of trust Preston put in Rick.

Rick described how the money would be taped up in Tide detergent boxes and on one occasion, Rick needed gas money, so Preston instructed him to open the Tide box and grab one of the bundles. Rick said the bundle he grabbed had $1,000 in it, and he assumed all the bundles had $1,000 in them, but this large Tide box was filled with these bundles.

The significance of the Tide detergent boxes was to mask the smell of the drug money in case Rick was stopped during the trip.

Rick thought of one other thing that might be significant to us regarding the day those three bodies were found on fire up north. He said Preston called him to meet that day. Rick said this call came in the morning, which was unusual because Preston normally called in the afternoon.

Rick said Preston was driving a maroon Chevy Monte Carlo with Gaylan, and they asked him to drive a U-Haul truck for them, which he agreed to do.

Rick got into the Monte Carlo, and they drove to a new neighborhood in the northwest part of town that had several houses under construction. When they arrived at a house that was still under construction, Rick saw a U-Haul truck parked in the driveway, at which time, Preston threw Rick the keys and told him to follow them. Rick said they drove around for a while with him just following them, and it did not appear as if they were driving to any specific location.

Preston called Rick on his cell phone and asked him if they could take the truck to Rick's house in southeast Omaha. He agreed with no questions asked. Rick said they took the truck to his house and parked it in the backyard, and he was driven back to his pickup truck and then they separated.

Later that day, Rick said Gaylan arrived at his house with a new truck, which was a cube truck that looked just like a U-Haul, but was painted white. With Gaylan was "Little Chuck," Chuck Nissan's son, who is a small nineteen-year-old black kid who grew up on Fortieth Avenue in his grandmother's house because his dad was always running the streets or in prison.

Little Chuck was also in the car with Preston the day he was arrested during the original search warrants. Little Chuck had been transported to central station and interviewed, but there was no reason to hold him. His real name was identified at that time as Zach Woods. This now would be the second time in this investigation that Zach Woods's name came up.

Rick described how the two trucks were parked back to back in the alley. When the truck doors were opened up, the U-Haul truck was filled with bales of marijuana. The bales of marijuana were moved from the U-Haul truck to the white truck. Rick said it was his estimation that there was well over 2,000 pounds of marijuana moved from one truck to the other.

Rick told us Gaylan asked if the white truck could be kept at his house for a while and Rick agreed. Then Gaylan and Little Chuck left. Rick said this truck sat in his back yard for nearly two weeks until Preston contacted him to bring the truck to a new business, which was their lawn service business front.

This time sequence was crucial because it was not until after the murders that Preston and Gaylan obtained the property for the lawn service business front.

Rick also described how in this same time period he was requested to take possession of several guns and ammunition from Preston. These guns were previously stored at a house Preston and Gaylan had maintained in the south part of Omaha as a stash house for a period of time, but they had stopped using this house.

Rick still had the ammunition that was given to him, but the guns had either been given back to Preston or he was instructed to take them to the Arizona house. Rick also said Preston instructed him to melt down two of the guns with a torch. So Rick did, while Preston watched him melt the guns, telling him the pieces were not small enough as he was breaking up the guns.

About three days before Preston's arrest, Rick was instructed to go to Phoenix to get a 300-pound load of marijuana. Once he arrived in Phoenix, he went to Preston's new house in Avondale, Arizona, and took possession of the 300 pounds, then started driving back to Omaha, waiting until he heard from Preston.

On the day of the raids, which was April 4, Rick received a call from Preston to meet him at the house on Fortieth Avenue with the marijuana. Rick then received a follow-up call not to go to the Fortieth Avenue house because the police were there.

Preston called Rick again to meet at the Crown Storage Units, but Preston forgot his keys in Arizona, so he wanted Rick to bring his torch. Preston then called a third time, changing the meet location to a Perkins restaurant.

Rick believed this was a play by Preston to make sure he was not being followed by the cops because Preston watched Rick arrive at the restaurant. After this cat and mouse game, they finally hooked up at the Perkins restaurant, where Preston instructed Rick to follow him, looking to see if Rick was setting him up or being followed by cops.

Once Preston was satisfied that the coast was clear, he said to Rick, "Follow me."

"I followed Shine north on Seventy-Second Street, and I saw the cops swoop in on him as he was approaching Crown Storage," Rick said. "I'm shitting my pants, so I just turn off at the next street and got out of there. I took the marijuana home and just sat tight."

Rick stated a couple days later, he got a call from a guy claiming to be Preston's brother, and Rick was supposed to give him what he was holding for Shine. Rick told him he needed to hear that from Shine himself.

A short time later, Rick received a three-way call from Preston through Yessica instructing him to give all those "petitions," which was a code word for the marijuana, to his brother, so that was what Rick did. He turned the marijuana over to Shine's brother, who was Lavarius Blade.

A couple of weeks later, Rick was again contacted by Preston on a three-way call from jail, asking Rick if all the petitions were turned over to his brother. Rick said he sensed from this question that Preston's brother must have ripped Shine off, saying that he didn't get all the marijuana from Rick.

At the conclusion of this interview, we then changed locations to Rick's residence, where he escorted us inside and took us to a white plastic bag that contained numerous boxes, magazines, and loose ammunition of various calibers and types. In the bottom of this bag were four loose .44-caliber Smith & Wesson rounds, in addition to a box that contained thirty-three .44-caliber Smith & Wesson, 200-grain, Gold Dot hollow-point rounds.

This recovery was extremely significant because nearly a year earlier, after the autopsies of the three burned bodies, when the bullet fragments were recovered, they were turned over to a ballistics expert in the crime lab.

During the analysis of these bullet fragments, which was completed by measuring and weighing the bullet fragments and comparing the fragments to known manufactured specifications of ammunition, a potential list was created of what type of ammunition these bullet fragments came from. This was actually very technical, calculated by using a microscope and measuring weights in grain quantities.

Ultimately, the pool of suspected ammunition these bullet fragments came from was narrowed down to only four specific types of ammunition. Considering all the types of ammunition that are available in the world, narrowing it down to four is fairly amazing.

Wouldn't you know it, but a year earlier, one of the types of ammunition listed was Smith & Wesson .44-caliber 200 grain Gold Dot hollow point with crimping. Crimping is the pinching down of the bullet to the actual shell casing. This was an exact match to the type of ammunition we had now recovered from Rick, who retrieved it from Preston.

This was great information. It was another nail in the coffin, as they say. When this evidence would be presented to a jury someday, it would definitely leave an impression.

After talking to Rick Ginney, we updated the chart.

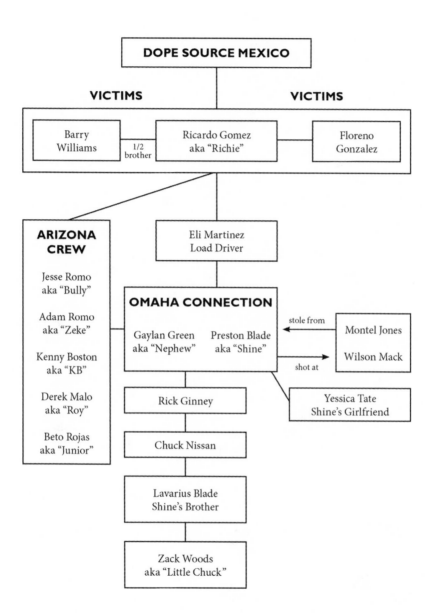

39
JAIL CALLS

After this interview with Rick Ginney and his statements regarding the three-way telephone calls he had while Preston Blade was incarcerated, it was apparent that the jail calls of both Preston and Gaylan needed to be reviewed. This is a common procedure and tactic used during investigations; however, just because of the quantity of follow-up being conducted up until this time, we had not yet listened to any calls.

To clarify, in the county correctional facility where Preston and Gaylan were being housed, the inmates have access to purchase telephone time. At the beginning of every telephone call, an automated recording tells the inmate the telephone call is being recorded and is subject to monitoring. By this time, nearly sixty days of phone calls had been recorded on our two bad guys.

In a perfect world, it would have been nice to listen to the calls shortly after they happened, but it was not realistic in this investigation, and now we were very far behind. A jail call can last up to fifteen minutes per call before it is automatically shut off with no limit to the number of calls an inmate can make per day, as long as the inmate has money on his phone account, which is paid for by family and friends.

As Roscoe and I began the process of listening to jail calls, literally hundreds of phone calls had been completed. Unfortunately, Roscoe was assigned to another homicide investigation, which left the phone call review solely on my shoulders.

If an investigator does the phone call reviewing process properly, he or she starts at the beginning to learn the context of each conversation and how the conversations are inter-related with details from previous conversations.

If an officer just picks and chooses different conversations from the pool of recorded calls indiscriminately, that officer may miss detailed information that references previous conversations. It had to be done, even though we were still swamped with follow-up during this case.

I convinced Sgt. Bogowski to let me get the calls downloaded onto CDs so I could review them at home. This was a perfect scenario. My wife, Rae, was working midnights, supervising a uniform patrol crew, so when she left for work and the kids were in bed, I would begin to listen to jail phone calls at our house.

This process continued over the next two and a half months. I'd listen to four hours of calls a night, sleep for four hours, then get up and go to work the next day. The process was painstaking, but would be fruitful.

Within the first few days of reviewing phone calls, I located the telephone calls described by Rick Ginney regarding use of the term *petitions* as code for marijuana and Preston inquiring if all the petitions had been turned over to his brother.

Numerous conversations were heard between Preston and Yessica, describing how Preston's brother, Lavarius, was not trustworthy and he had not made all the payments to Yessica for the last load, which, if based on Rick's number of 300 pounds, could actually have a street value of $300,000.

Yessica also spoke about other people stopping by the house with money, making payments from "work" that was already out on the street. This, I believed, was in reference to marijuana that had been fronted to people prior to Preston's arrest.

Fronting is a term used in the drug dealing trade, which is a process in which the drug (in this case, marijuana) is supplied to somebody and the payment is made later after it is sold. In real terms, it is kind of like a doper-world line of credit.

One of the most exciting calls came when Preston called Yessica just after she was victimized in the home invasion. She was really upset and crying, nearly hysterical. Numerous calls contained this subject matter, trying to figure out who the intruders were. But most interestingly was the fact that Yessica reported to Preston that $30,000 was taken that night, when she had told the cops nothing was taken.

Another person who was repeatedly mentioned in many calls was referred to as "Little Man." It was apparent from the conversations between Preston and Yessica that Little Man was somebody Preston considered a liability. Preston repeatedly asked Yessica if she had seen Little Man and then told Yessica when she does see Little Man, tell him to "keep his mouth shut, they have nothing but a little weed."

As these "Little Man" calls evolved, it certainly seemed that this person would be a key in discovering some damaging information on Preston. There was another person spoken of often, whom Preston and Yessica referred to as "Uncle J," who was also a concern to Preston, but it seemed his level of concern was not as high as it was with Little Man.

Eventually, a comment was made about Uncle J living across the street, which triggered my recollection of the search warrants and the neighbor across the street whom Yessica went to on the date of the warrants. This neighbor was Johnny Baustau. Although, this was only a calculated guess on my part, I at least had someone to look at when the time came.

One of the most shocking and notable pieces of information developed from calls made by Preston to a woman with the nickname of "Ro." At first it seemed that Ro was just another girlfriend Preston had on the side. I sensed she must have been close to Preston because she was visiting him in jail, and they would talk about the visits during some of the phone calls. They talked about the revealing clothing she was wearing during these visits and how Preston wanted her to keep wearing the revealing clothing.

These statements regarding revealing clothing and possible personal contact did not seem logical to me because policy within the jail prohibited actual person-to-person contacts. Visitation was done by a video phone system.

My thought process soon changed during one of the calls when the personal relationship conversation and banter moved into more of a legal jargon conversation. I thought to myself, *No way could this be the attorney, Rolinda Dupree?* I thought if it was Rolinda Dupree, why in the world would they be talking on an open line when, as an attorney, she would have access to the attorney-client privilege and could talk on a private line that law enforcement could not monitor.

Before I could complete a subpoena to verify if the phone number Preston was calling belonged to Rolinda Dupree, Preston's personality and leadership skills began to take over. Preston gave Ro detailed instructions on contacting potential witnesses in this case and telling these witnesses that ass-kickings would be given if they cooperated with authorities.

During this recorded phone conversation, Ro was doing her best to keep Preston quiet and not allow him to make any of these statements on the phone, but it was apparent that Preston was becoming frustrated by his incarceration and could not stay in control.

I quickly confirmed by subpoena that the phone number was, in fact, Rolinda Dupree and these conversations were between an attorney and a client. This entire situation was so stupid on both of their parts, specifically for Rolinda, because she was protected by the attorney-client privilege and could have had her phone number blocked and calls not recorded, but she chose not to for some reason. All she had to do was identify her phone number to the correctional facility's administration and they would have blocked any recordings of phone calls that went to her phone number.

Now that I had listened to these attorney-client phone conversations and had determined that there was content regarding witness intimidation, it was determined to continue to review these conversations regardless of the attorney-client privileges, based on the threats and intimidations that had already been monitored.

During the progression of the court proceedings, the prosecution is responsible for turning over discovery items for the defense to review. In this investigation, we specifically chose not to have an open file policy. In an open file policy, all reports and all evidence are turned over immediately for the defense to review. By choosing not to maintain an open file, the prosecution turned over a great deal of the evidence, however some was held back.

Specifically, what evidence was held back during the early stages of the discovery process were those interviews with key witnesses prior to trial. This information was held back for the most obvious reason: witness safety. Based on these previous jail phone calls, we knew that one of the defense tactics trying to be employed by Preston Blade was witness intimidation.

However, during the release of discovery, we turned over all information regarding our monitoring of jail phone calls. This release included Preston's monitored calls to Rolinda Dupree. No surprise after this release: Rolinda Dupree never showed up to another hearing.

Now as I think back about those in-person jail visits that took place between Rolinda and Preston, I think probably much more than legal counseling was taking place in the attorney-client room where client and attorney can meet face to face, so to speak. I guess that interaction—and her revealing clothing—gives a whole new meaning to the attorney-client privilege.

As a result of the interview with Rick and the review of jail phone calls, I planned on another round of superseding indictments at the next grand jury meeting. This time we added Chuck Nissan, Yessica Tate, Rick Ginney, and Lavarius Blade on marijuana charges.

I hoped this next round of indictments would increase anxiety and develop a witness to the triple homicide. I had anticipated that Yessica would surely be interested in the discovery information regarding the jail calls between Preston and Rolinda. One can never underestimate a scorned co-conspirator and girlfriend.

We also began to review Gaylan Green's phone calls, but it was apparent just from the downloading of calls, he only made a few calls. In reviewing these initial calls, Gaylan primarily spoke with his mother, who definitely presented herself as a wise person, giving Gaylan instructions not to talk on the phone and only engage in conversations regarding the case with her in person. All in all, from a legal standpoint, good advice from his mother.

Before the end of this case, I listened to and documented over five hundred jail calls primarily involving Preston. During this process, I used some of the interactions between Preston and Yessica as a parental tool in my personal life. During many calls, Yessica would be at home with her two children and the household seemed chaotic and unruly, with Yessica screaming to the children, "I'm gonna put a whoopin' on you."

I, in turn, played this quote to my children and explained to them how lucky they were in this world. I guess in hindsight, by listening to all these jail phone calls, we did, in a sense, do our wiretap on Preston after all.

Ultimately, only a handful of these hundreds of phone calls were used during the trial. They were transcribed exactly onto paper, so the jury could read along as the tapes were being played—driving yet another nail in the coffin.

40
SMILE!
YOU'RE ON CAMERA

I was only getting four hours of sleep a night, but the case was still very active. I was hoping that during one of the jail calls, Preston Blade or Gaylan Green would talk about the murders. Now remember, I said the media correlated the two cases, so Preston and Gaylan knew we were getting close. I just hoped one of them would say something.

Then, out of the blue, in the middle of June, prior to Yessica's indictment, she called me, "Mr. H, I need to get them cameras back. Those cameras you took out of my apartment."

As she said that, I thought, *Fuck, I haven't gotten to those cameras yet.*

I politely told her, "I can't release any items yet because the investigation is still in progress."

As soon as I hung up the phone, I realized we had not yet looked at the cameras. This is usually done right away for three reasons. First, so you don't forget to do it; second, to develop evidence. It is common for people involved in the illegal narcotics business to take trophy pictures of their money and their dope. It happens all the time. And third, not that we cops are a bunch of perverts, but it is not uncommon to find some level of home adult video entertainment.

As I looked back, I'm sure that I had this task of developing and reviewing the film in all the cameras on one of my daily to-do lists at one time, but somehow it slipped through the cracks. So I dropped everything, went down to the property/evidence room, and located all the cameras taken into evidence, which also included a camcorder.

The review and retrieval of what was on these cameras was not something I trusted myself to do. With my luck, I would erase whatever was on it, so I called the audio-visual tech guy at the U.S. Attorney's office—another one of my experts—a retired military man, who could navigate technical audio-visual and computer things as easy as it was for me to take a breath.

Within an hour, I was at his office and we were searching the cameras. In my wildest dreams, I would not have imagined what was on the camcorder.

Preston was the cameraman, turning the camera on himself just to confirm that he was the narrator of this home video (thank you). The video then panned to Gaylan sitting at a card table inside the garage of the lawn service business. On the table was a mountain of money, which Gaylan was counting and organizing. Also on the table, in clear view, was at least a one-gallon Ziploc bag full of what appeared to be marijuana.

Preston even joked on the tape, "Look at all this shit. We don't owe any motherfucker anything. What we got is ours."

Preston then panned the camera throughout the garage and started to display their collection of vehicles, specifically, the two BMWs, the Corvette, the Magnums, and the Suburbans. During this video, the two of them were laughing and having a great time expressing how wonderful life is.

As if Preston knew we would someday see this video, he zoomed in on the Ziploc bag, presumably a pound of marijuana, and said, "Hey Mr. Policeman, if you ever see this tape, that ain't weed, that's just a little bit of sage."

Then both guys laughed hysterically.

I figured this video would be huge at some point later in the jury trial. Just what the hardworking, taxpaying jury member wants to see—these guys living it up on dope money.

I finally located the jail phone call that corresponded with the request by Preston for Yessica to ask me for the video cameras. Preston told Yessica to try to get the cameras back because there might be something on them.

I plotted two separate timelines for the prosecutions in this case: one telling how events unfolded in chronological order and the second sequence on the investigative timeline, which showed how the events, in real time, were actually discovered in the investigative process.

41
BIG NEWS
ABOUT LITTLE MAN

The federal grand jury meets on the third week of every month to hear testimony for indictments. Assistant U.S. Attorney Lillian Lomax decided to present the additional suspects for indictment at this time—a year after the bodies were found burning in the wooded area.

The federal grand jury is the same group of people who meet for an eighteen-month period so the presentation of this evidence to them was not new. They had already heard testimony two months earlier regarding the first indictment of Preston "Shine" Blade and Gaylan "Nephew" Green and then again during the first superseding indictment adding additional charges, money and property. Now they were hearing more evidence.

We planned to add Yessica Tate because of her involvement in continuing the conspiracy, which was confirmed by her own voice on the jail calls, not to mention the recovery of evidence that was already in police custody regarding the camcorder.

We also planned to add Rick Ginney, based on his own admissions as the load driver; Chuck Nissan, based on Rick's statements and phone calls in which Chuck calls Yessica about dropping money off after Preston was already incarcerated; and Lavarius Blade, Preston's brother, who ripped him off, based on Rick's statements and phone calls talking about the last load being taken by Lavarius and his lack of payment to Yessica.

Isn't that beautiful? Two dope-dealing brothers, one ripping the other off.

After the indictments were approved by the grand jury, arrest warrants did not become active for a few days. While waiting for the arrest warrants, I wrote additional search warrants on two locations still being used by Yessica because she was actively collecting money on marijuana that was on the street prior to Preston's arrest.

During this warrant sweep, Yessica was arrested and two significant items were located. One was a large medallion necklace studded with countless diamonds spelling out the words "Deuce's Down." This was the same name as the recording studio that Preston and Gaylan had started. This necklace was appraised at over $25,000.

Yessica was also wearing large diamond earrings at the time of her arrest, which were also seized as evidence.

Also, Yessica was now driving another car, a fairly new Buick Rendezvous, which she paid $12,700 for thirty days earlier. Yessica was starting to get wise to our ways though. She purchased this car through her grandmother and put it in her grandmother's name.

We still took custody of the SUV, believing we could prove it was only in the grandmother's name, but actually purchased by Yessica with drug money. We did follow-up interviews with the car dealership and located jail phone calls that clearly talked about putting the vehicle in the grandmother's name for protection.

After Yessica's arrest, she was appointed legal counsel. As a result of this legal counsel, arrangements were quickly made for Yessica to give a proffer statement. The results of this interview could be beneficial for both parties. Yessica could certainly get substantial reductions in her sentence if her information was valuable.

I certainly believed she was close enough to Preston and Gaylan that not only would she have dope information, but I also thought she would have been involved in conversation about the murders after the fact, especially after all the pressure we had applied and the media coverage.

At the first interview at the U.S. Attorney's office, all the proper formalities were completed. We outlined the proffer statement and agreement. It was now time to talk.

But Yessica began to cry, quickly becoming hysterical, acting as if she can't breathe. I looked at the attorneys and asked if she needed a rescue squad, but I was actually thinking she just needed better acting lessons.

Yessica's attorney requested time to speak with her in private to change the course of events. I was okay with that, but I was also realistic that she didn't want to play ball. So be it. I still had a lot of work to do. After about fifteen minutes of coddling, Yessica's attorney came out of the room and said she was ready.

As we began, I tried to be as gentle as possible:

"Can you tell me about how you and Preston first got together?" I started asking easy questions about her history with Preston.

She told us they were having kids and about the houses. She had a separate apartment out of the hood, paying $8 a month for a subsidized apartment in Papillion, a suburb south of Omaha.

Things began to flow with interaction going back and forth during the questioning, but I really had not asked any hard questions yet.

I thought the best way to transition into the hard questions was to bring up the recorded jail calls, which I had copies of. Specifically, I asked, "What did you mean when you told Preston that $30,000 was taken during the home invasion, when you told the police nothing was taken?"

Yessica answered, "I lied to the police that night. There really was $30,000 taken."

My obvious next question was, "Where did the $30,000 come from?" thinking she would answer that it was marijuana debt payments owed to Preston. But, oh no.

Yessica described it this way, "One of Nephew's family members brought me $50,000 shortly after Shine and Nephew's arrest to help me get by until the boys are out of jail."

At first I thought, *Bullshit,* but I quickly remembered a jail call where Preston asked Yessica if "G's people" brought that "fifty" by. When I originally heard that, I thought it was either $50 or $50 worth of weed, certainly not $50,000 cash. This would account for the funds on the Buick Rendezvous.

As the questions continued to a more criminal nature about drug deals and murder conversations, Yessica began to get upset again, so the interview ended. We did try a couple more times to speak with Yessica at the request of her attorney, who always had the best interest of Yessica in mind, but it always ended the same with Yessica crying and saying she was the victim.

Rick Ginney turned himself in with a phone call and was actually granted a status of non-incarceration prior to trial. That left Chuck Nissan and Lavarius Blade. Lavarius was run on local television's *Crime Stoppers,* which led to his quick arrest. He chose not to cooperate and pled guilty to the conspiracy to distribute marijuana fairly quickly.

Chuck Nissan got a little nervous after we went to the Fortieth Avenue block and put out the word we were looking for him. So what did he do but call me and gave me a great admission over the phone. He wanted to make it clear that he only made one run of 120 pounds of marijuana, nothing more.

Chuck was fearful about turning himself in, but was finally arrested when an anonymous caller gave the location where Chuck was hiding. He was arrested without incident and wouldn't you know it? He had a pound of marijuana at the house where we grabbed him.

Chuck gave his own proffer statement, which described all the relationships among himself, Rick Ginney, and Preston Blade. Chuck also described the relationship that his son, Zach Woods, had with Preston, also confirming that his son had the nicknames of "Little Chuck" and "Little Man."

This was a huge piece of information because during the jail calls, Preston talked about Little Man and had all the concern and worry for Little Man as a liability, specifically not wanting him to talk. I didn't know what Preston was worried about with Little Man, but I was sure going to find out.

Roscoe and I made a stop at Little Man's grandmother's house on the Fortieth Avenue block and left a business card with her, asking him to call us.

42
THE YELLOW HOUSE

It was now early August. After the last round of indictments, I continued to listen to jail phone calls, although I was losing ground, getting farther and farther behind. In a somewhat mundane phone call between Preston and Yessica, normal conversation was taking place. But in the middle of this conversation, a new name came up: Lincoln. The reference was very quick and Preston said he was not worried about him because he would never say anything.

This statement certainly alerted me as unusual; however, I didn't really know what it meant. I thought to myself, *How many Lincoln names could there be in the county computer mainframe.* If the number was reasonable, I would track them all down.

Well, not only was the number reasonable, it was downright small. There were only four people in the county mainframe with the first name of Lincoln, and one of those was actually dead, so that left three names to follow up to see if there was a relationship in some way to Preston Blade.

Within a day, I used the addresses listed on the Lincoln names just to drive by the locations and plan when I would follow up with interviews.

The first address did not ring a bell, but as I drove to the house and pulled up near the house, my jaw nearly hit the steering wheel.

The house was directly next door to the barber shop in the strip mall that Preston and Gaylan had run. I certainly should have noticed that address as I read the paperwork, but there again is the factor of human error and my low IQ.

I drove past the barber shop and pulled up right in front of this house. It matched exactly to the location described by the load driver, Eli Martinez, as the location where he dropped off the marijuana.

I knew right away this location could be key. Remember, we were still looking for the actual murder scene, so now I was eager to research the history of this property. I quickly identified the owners and met with them the next day.

During this interview, the owners gave me information for the current renters and identified the previous occupant as Lincoln Coolidge. The property owner then described an unusual event that happened during Lincoln's occupancy at this house: Lincoln recarpeted the living room on his own accord.

The property owner said this was strange for two reasons; first, no renter *ever* recarpets the property they are renting, and second, new carpet had been installed in the house just prior to Lincoln taking possession of this place.

I researched Lincoln Coolidge's current whereabouts and learned that he was in jail on gun charges in the federal prison in Leavenworth, Kansas. So off Roscoe and I went to Leavenworth. And, yes, they do have Waffle Houses in Kansas. Within a day of finding out about this house and Lincoln's association with it, we were sitting with Lincoln Coolidge in an interview room.

We began by identifying ourselves and explaining our purpose and our interest in his old address. We told him we thought a crime may have happened there.

"We're the guys investigating Shine," I said.

Without us asking any questions, Lincoln starts talking: "I rented that house with my girlfriend. We lived there. We got in a fight, and she got a new house. After a few months, we made up, and I went to live with her in her place. In case we got another fight, I didn't want to let that house go. Shine was running that barber shop next door. I told him he could use it as a hangout as long as he paid all the bills. I turned the keys over to him, and I never had anything to do with that house."

Lincoln then speculated about the murders, "If it happened in that house, I had nothing to do with it, and my cousin told me he changed the carpet because he spilled something on it." It turns out Lincoln and Shine were distant cousins.

Even though we didn't think Lincoln was a suspect, but based on these initial statements, we decided to read Lincoln his Miranda rights because he was already in jail.

When I got to the final line of the Miranda warnings and said, "Do you want to have a lawyer with you during questioning?"

He said, "Maybe I should."

So he requested to have his attorney counsel him before he went any further. This was fine with us, so we made arrangements to meet again with his attorney the following week. However, when we arrived back at Leavenworth the following week, to our great surprise Lincoln had been transferred to a federal correctional facility in Oklahoma City, Oklahoma.

We then arranged a trip to Oklahoma City; however, Lincoln's attorney did not want to make this trip, so we arranged to have phone contact between the attorney and Lincoln in place when the interview occurred.

Once we organized this event and the interview began, Lincoln detailed his turning the property over to his cousin, Preston, around Christmas of 2004.

Lincoln said he had very little, if any, contact with that residence after he left. He was on the run for a federal probation violation by May 5—ironically, the day the bodies were found burning. Lincoln told us during this time on the run, he had some contact with Preston because that is how he learned about the carpet replacement, but he was pretty sure the contact did not happen at the house and possibly happened on the street.

Although Lincoln added nothing new to what he told us earlier, the key for us was that Lincoln put control of that house in Shine's hands.

At the end of this interview, while sitting in the parking lot of the federal prison, my cell phone rang. Zach "Little Man" Woods was on the line.

Little Man was nineteen, a black kid, raised by his grandmother, mainly on the Fortieth Avenue block, surrounded by gang violence and street-level drug activity, yet he did not even have a criminal record. And here he was calling me back. I liked him already.

Zach said to me, "I heard you wanted to talk to me. What about?"

I then went into my spiel about my thoughts that he had information about the case I was working. I told Zach that he had not been indicted, but I knew he was very close to Preston and Gaylan and I believed he had information that would be damaging to them.

Zach politely said, "I don't want to piss you off, but I don't want nuthin to do with Shine or Nephew or their situation."

I definitely could sense Zach was scared. And why wouldn't he be? He was a kid, a small kid. He had no money, his grandmother lived on the Fortieth Avenue block, and I was asking him to provide information on two giant, multi-million-dollar drug dealers who I thought killed three people.

Yeah, I guess he had every right to be scared. I went so far with Zach in this phone call that I did something I had never done before. I told him if he talked to me truthfully now, I would not indict him on any drug charges that could ever be developed in this case. But ultimately, after a forty-five-minute conversation, it ended with Zach respectfully saying he was not interested, and I really couldn't blame him.

It was time to add Lincoln Coolidge to the chart.

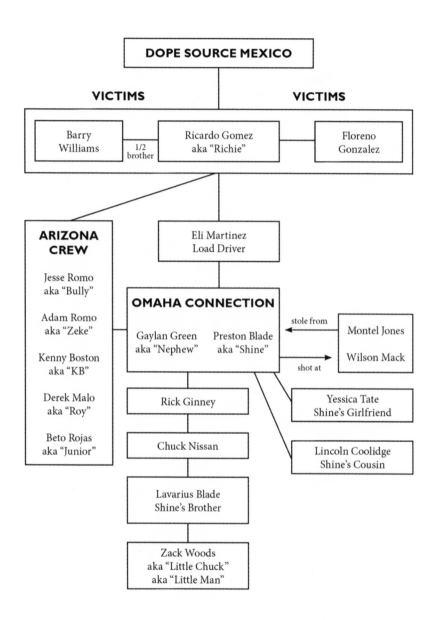

43
DIRTY TRASH

It had now reached mid-August. Roscoe and I were back from Oklahoma City. Lincoln Coolidge's old house was looking really good as the next logical step in this investigation to look for a possible murder scene.

I was also trying to sell Lilly Lomax on an indictment for Zach Woods (Little Man). We knew he was in the car with Preston when he was arrested on April 4, and we had Rick Ginney's statements regarding the marijuana transfer from the U-Haul to the white truck involving Zach. We also had the jail calls where Preston was concerned about Little Man talking and the statements from Chuck Nissan, identifying Little Man as his son.

Lilly agreed with this next indictment, but only if Rick Ginney would positively identify a photograph of Zach Woods as Little Man as being the kid who was involved in the transfer of the marijuana from the U-Haul to the white truck.

That seemed like a simple enough request but, remember, Zach Woods had no criminal history so that meant there was no mug shot on file for him. He also did not have a driver's license, so there was no photo of him with the Department of Motor Vehicles.

But I remembered that Zach was in the car with Preston on April 4 when Preston was arrested in the area of the Crown Storage Units. Zach was also transported to police headquarters and placed in an interview room for several hours that day before he was interviewed and released.

I checked out the video copy of that interview, took it to Crime Lab Technician Sonny Buvano and asked if he could produce a still-frame photo from this videotape, which he quickly did.

After getting it cleared with Rick's attorney who now represented him in the federal indictment, I called Rick who was still free on a release status, which always concerned me for two reasons. First, it gave Rick the opportunity to get himself in trouble by making a stupid decision, either using drugs or committing some crime, which will actually hurt his credibility in court. But even more worrisome was the fact that he could get killed or intimidated while out on the street.

Even though we had not officially released our statements from co-conspirators in discovery, it did not take a rocket scientist to figure out who the likely witnesses were in the cast of characters, and Preston definitely knew the people who were liabilities to him. At the top of the list were Rick and Little Man.

I met Rick where he was working, showed him the picture, and asked if he knew who the person was in the photograph, not giving him any indicators. Without any hesitation, Rick said, "Sure I do. That's Chuck Nissan's son. They call him Little Chuck or Little Man."

Rick told me he's known him his entire life, and Little Man helped him transfer the load of marijuana at his house from the U-Haul truck to the white cube truck that Gaylan had brought over.

Rick told us about the many times when he was at the lawn service business front and Little Man would show up and pick up five- and ten-pound quantities of marijuana from Preston. Rick said on one occasion, Zach showed up with a stranger and Preston went off on Little Man for bringing a new person around. Rick described how Preston always liked Zach and would boast how Preston took better care of Zach than Chuck, Zach's own father, did.

This is exactly what I needed. The pressure would soon be applied to Zach "Little Man" Woods.

Things were going well with Rick Ginney, so just off the cuff, I asked him what knowledge he had of Preston's neighbor, Johnny Baustau.

Rick asked, "You mean Johnny, who lives right across the street?" I nodded my head. Rick described Johnny as a good old boy, who would do odd jobs for Shine.

Rick said Shine had a lot of trust in Johnny because at least three times Preston was not around or back from Arizona when Rick arrived with the load, so he contacted Shine who told him to call Johnny across the street. Johnny had keys to Preston's house on Fortieth Avenue and would let Rick in the rear garage door where the two of them would unload the marijuana, which averaged 500 pounds per load.

Holy cow! This was too good. Did I dare push my luck by inquiring about Lincoln Coolidge's house? Well, of course I did.

So next I asked a vague question to Rick to see if he would give a detailed answer. I asked, "Do you know of any other properties related to Preston or Gaylan in the area of the barber shop they once had?"

Without hesitation, Rick responded, "Hell, yeah, Shine had a yellow house right next door." Rick then talked about how he, on a couple occasions, met Shine there to pick up what Rick called "dirty trash."

"What do you mean by dirty trash?" I asked.

He explained they were the bale wrappings from the marijuana loads, which contained the residue and crumbs of marijuana after breaking up the bales and repackaging them into one-pound packages. Rick said he would take these bale wrappings to his house and shake them out on a tarp and, by doing this, he could actually yield between a half to a pound of marijuana just from the trash.

Rick then dropped a bomb on me. He said, "I laid some carpet in that house for Shine."

Rick recalled that he picked up the carpet from White's Carpet Mart, located at Fortieth and Hamilton Streets. Rick said he believed this took place just a few weeks after the burning bodies had been found. The carpet had already been paid for, he just picked it up and took it to the yellow house next to the barber shop.

"I take it to the house. I go in, and the house just reeked, stunk," he told us. "It was so bad, I had to go back to my house to get a fan to air it out for a couple days before I could lay that carpet."

"What kind of flooring did you put the carpet on?" I asked.

"Oak flooring," he said. "There was definitely fresh water stains on it."

Rick then asked me a question, "Do you think it happened there?"

I politely said, "I don't know," but in my mind I was thinking, *No shit, Sherlock.*

I contacted Roscoe about this latest interaction, and he went to White's Carpet Mart right away and recovered a contract on the carpet purchase in the name of U-A-F Lawns, signed by Gaylan on May 9, 2005, just five days after the murders.

I then asked Rick Ginney if he could break away from his work for a few minutes so we could confirm the location where Johnny lived for identification purposes. He then directed me to Johnny's house, which was right across the street from Preston and Yessica's house on Fortieth Avenue—a tiny clapboard house, like many in the neglected neighborhood, only this one was set back at the top of the hilly street, up a set of steep concrete steps.

I returned Rick to work at the junk yard, went directly to the police station, and created a photo lineup with one of the photos being Johnny Baustau. I drove back to Rick's workplace and showed him the photo lineup. He picked out Johnny Baustau as the Johnny who helped unload the three loads of marijuana.

We updated our chart to confirm the identities of Johnny Baustau and Zach Woods.

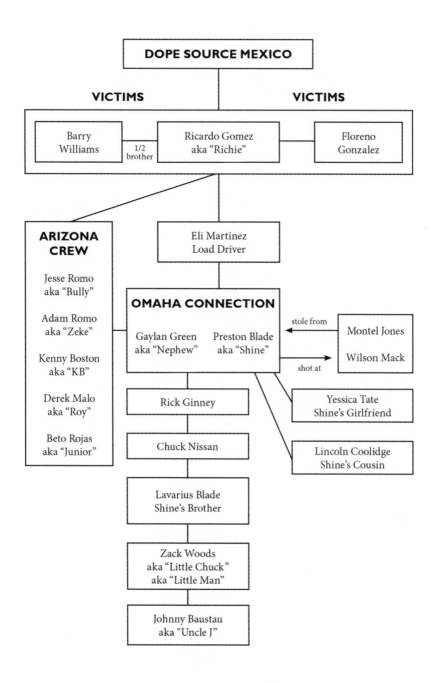

44
CLEAN-UP GUY

Zach Woods and Johnny Baustau were now subjects of the next grand jury indictments.

Once the arrest warrants were issued, it did not take long to get either one of them in custody. Once they were in custody, court-appointed attorneys were assigned to them, and by the end of August, both Zach and Johnny wanted to proffer.

I believed these proffers would be the critical ones. These were the two guys that Preston was worried about in his jail phone calls. I hoped both of these guys would give it up completely without holding anything back, but this process can be slow with the interviewee only giving up little pieces of information at a time.

I don't know why they do this, but they do. Even after the advice of their counsel and the reading of the rules in the proffer agreement, guys are always holding information back; they are always playing a never-ending game of strategy. But, then, so were we.

Zach Woods was first to go. We met in the interview room at the U.S. Attorney's office on the fourteenth floor of the old First National Bank building in downtown Omaha. His attorney was there.

Zach was rocking back and forth in the chair, his eyes jetting around the room, swallowing hard, and thinking hard about what's about to happen.

But he began to talk, describing his actions on the night of the murders. These initial statements were general and vague, but Zach did put himself at the murder scene when the gunshots were fired. However, Zach put himself outside the house, next to the barber shop during the shooting.

He saw the bodies. In fact, he helped load them into a truck before Preston and Gaylan took him back to the block on Fortieth Avenue.

In my role as the interviewer, I have to make many snap decisions at the time of the interview—whether to push forward or hold back, always trying to keep the individual talking, but reading their actions and mannerisms to determine how hard to push to keep the information flowing. I was sure that this initial statement, as vague as it was, had some strands of truth in it, but there had to be more details. I decided to push.

"You're full of shit," I fired back. Roscoe and I were way too wise to believe that Preston and Gaylan drove him back to the block on Fortieth Avenue with three bodies in the back of the truck so he didn't have any further involvement. That was a bunch of crap.

Zach then admitted he was actually at the site where they dumped the bodies and described it as only somebody who was there could.

"We drove from the house by the barber shop and went towards Twenty-Fourth Street and then we turned north and went a long way until there were no more houses," he started out.

"We turned into a number of drives and backed out, looking for the perfect spot to dump the bodies."

At this point I knew he had been there. This was a key description because it matched the physical evidence at the scene with the blood trails turning into the different inlets.

After they found the spot to dump the bodies, Zach said they backed the truck in, unloaded the bodies, and set them on fire.

They then went back to Shine's house on Fortieth Avenue. Shine told Zach to get Johnny across the street because Shine wanted him to clean something up. Zach said he went and got Johnny and told him to go over to Shine's house, but then he took off to his grandmother's house down the street, not wanting to be involved any more that night.

Zach was then asked to draw a diagram of the house next to the barber shop and show where the bodies were located when he saw them before they were loaded into the truck, which he did.

This initial statement from Zach definitely had pertinent information in it, but my gut feeling was there was a lot more. I figured after a few days in jail, Zach may become more talkative, so we ended the interview.

Next was Johnny Baustau, the neighbor who was in his forties. A black man from the South, he spoke with a slow drawl. When asked to tell his involvement with Preston and Gaylan, he didn't hesitate.

"On the night before the bodies was found and set on fire way up north," Johnny said, he was at his house on Fortieth Avenue sleeping. "Between 2:30 and 4 in the morning, there's a knock on the door. It was Little Man."

" 'Shine need you to clean something up. You can make some quick money,' Little Man told me," Johnny said.

Johnny got dressed and went outside, but did not see Shine on the street in front of the house, so he walked behind Shine's house to the rear garage, where he saw Preston and Gaylan standing around Gaylan's black truck.

Johnny told us, "Shine said, 'Do you wanna make some money, man?' and I said, Yah, what do I gotta do?"

"You gotta clean something up at the house by the shop," Shine said.

Johnny got in the truck with Shine and Nephew and they drove over to the house next to Shine's barber shop.

"So tell me what you see when you get to the house," I prompted him.

"We went inside through a side door by the carport. There was a bucket with ammonia water and a sponge," Johnny said. "Shine pointed to some stuff on the floor for me to clean up."

Johnny said the house was lit poorly with some type of utility lights, but he began to do as Shine had requested.

"I got on my hands and knees and started scrubbing the floor," Johnny said. Preston and Gaylan left in the black truck.

"I knew it was blood," he said. "It was on the doorway that was between the kitchen and laundry room and all across the kitchen floor. Something was dragged across the floor. There was blood on the steps down from the kitchen to the laundry room and in the living room on the carpet."

I'm thinking, *Holy shit, this is my crime scene. We've got to process this.*

He went on, "In the living room, there were these three big circles of blood."

"How big?" I asked.

He made a circle with his hands about fifteen inches across.

Johnny said, "I wasn't feeling good," after twenty minutes of cleaning.

"Was it the ammonia or the blood?" I asked.

"I don't know, but I stopped, and I went outside and sat on the stoop of the barber shop next door," he said.

Johnny said he was sitting on the low brick wall for only a few minutes, when Preston and Gaylan came back.

Johnny told Preston and Gaylan he could not do any more cleaning because of the smell, so they began to berate him, calling him a "bitch ass nigger" repeatedly in various ways.

Johnny said he just took the abuse for several minutes until Preston and Gaylan went back over to the house. Johnny told us he just sat on the stoop and watched as they entered the house.

"They're in there for a few minutes and them dudes are carrying out the couch that was in the living room. It was covered with blood," he described. "They had all the cushions and pillows and set it down on the driveway. They started hosing it down. I guess they were trying to get the blood off of it."

Johnny said the two then loaded the couch, cushions, and pillows into the truck and drove away.

Johnny said they returned after about thirty minutes without the couch and went back inside the house without saying anything to him.

"Then they start coming out again, and they got carpet rolled up, and they're putting it in the back of the truck," he told us. "I'm figuring it's the carpet from the living room that had the blood on it. After they get that loaded up, they drive away again."

Johnny said Preston and Gaylan were gone for another thirty minutes.

"Why didn't you leave? Get a ride outta there?" I asked him.

"I didn't have a ride. I was just waitin' for them to take me back on the block," Johnny said.

After their last return to the house, they again berated Johnny and told him to get in the truck. They started to drive back to the Fortieth Avenue block and, during this drive, Gaylan gave Johnny $500 for his portion of the cleanup, but told him he would have gotten a lot more if he would have finished the job.

Johnny said by the time he got home, the morning news was starting to come on the television. "And the television is saying there's some brush fire north of town on Sixtieth Street. I remember that. Than a little while later, the newsman changes it from a brush fire to three bodies on fire. I knew right away them bodies on fire had something to do with Shine and Nephew."

Johnny then stated over the next several days and weeks, he spoke with Preston on the block of Fortieth Avenue, with Preston telling him, "Those Mexicans were from the cartel and they cannot be connected to us, so keep your mouth shut, and if you don't, anyone can come up missing."

Johnny said he was not looking for any trouble, so he went along with not saying anything. Johnny said he has always felt or sensed that Preston and Gaylan had been keeping their eye on him. Johnny knew in his mind, if the authorities asked, he was going to tell the truth, but he wasn't looking for trouble, so he wasn't saying anything until he was asked.

After these interviews, Zach and Johnny were taken back to the county correctional facility. We had a new problem to deal with. We now had multiple conspirators in the same facility, so arrangements were made to move Preston and Gaylan to other correctional facilities in the general area to prevent contact between co-conspirators and intimidation against future witnesses.

45
BLOOD WOULD BE NICE

Up until this point in the journey, a great narcotics conspiracy had been put together, developed and researched; but the murders, even with the statements of Zach Woods and Johnny Baustau, still needed some physical evidence to seal the deal.

All during this investigative process, I would stop into the County Attorney's office and keep Georgeann Goldstein in the loop. Even as good as it was going, she would always bring me back to reality by saying, "A little physical evidence, like some blood at a murder scene or something like that, would be nice."

I had been trying during this entire investigation to provide that. To this point, we had processed every possible vehicle (the U-Haul, the black truck now blue with a new bed liner) used to transport the bodies with negative results. We had processed the barber shop with no luck. No blood. No ties to the murder scene.

This would likely be our last shot at physical evidence—the processing of Lincoln Coolidge's house next door to the barber shop.

Based on Zach Woods's statement, even though I thought he was holding back, this was the murder scene, and based on Johnny Baustau's statement, there was great effort to destroy any evidence left there. In hindsight, I am actually surprised the house wasn't burned down, just like the bodies were set on fire.

Well, the house wasn't burned down, so, *What did we need to do?* I thought to myself. First, we needed to make contact with the renters who were living there. During this contact, Roscoe and I were going to have to explain to them that we needed to take possession of their house to look for forensic evidence of a crime that took place before they ever moved in.

"You can sign a permission-to-search form and voluntarily let us take control of your house for at least a week," I told this young couple. "We'd do a search that could be quite intrusive. We might remove carpet or wood flooring. If you choose this route, the government would put you up in a hotel, pay for your meals, and we will repair all damages we did to your house." That was their first option.

The alternative was something else. "I could write a search warrant, serve it to you, and you would have to fend for yourselves during the time period that we are in control of the house," I offered.

After I explained these two possibilities as politely as possible, our occupants eagerly took the free hotel and food. I had made contact with my FBI buddy, who came up with $2,000 to get these people out of the house and fix all the damages created during the search.

The first thing we did after getting the occupants out was to rent a storage pod and had it delivered to the house on the morning of September 3. Crime Lab Tech Sonny Buvano was assigned to be with us the entire week.

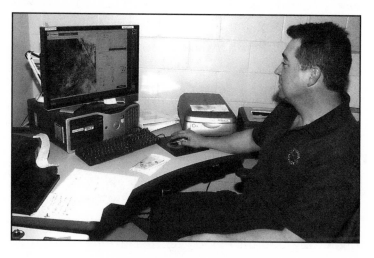

Sonny Buvano in the Crime Lab.

Before we began moving everything out, he took pictures of the house with all the furniture in place, so we knew what it looked like when we had to return everything at the end of our search. After all the furniture was removed, pictures were then taken how the house looked without furniture.

We began the process by bringing Zach Woods and Johnny Baustau, separately, to the house to point out what they had observed in relationship to the blood and bodies so many months earlier.

Then we began a close inspection of the kitchen and laundry room. During this inspection, it appeared that Johnny did not do a very good job of cleaning the woodwork or the door jamb between the kitchen and laundry room. With the naked eye, we could see dark brown smears on the woodwork, one of which was actually chunky and had some density to it. This was seventeen months after the murders. *Could we really be seeing what we thought was blood at our murder scene?*

We marked these spots with evidence markers, took photographs, swabbed the substance, and cut out the entire section of woodwork and made it a piece of evidence. This entire process was photographed.

During the next phase in the search, we took plenty of other swabs from other pieces of woodwork in the kitchen and laundry room area. We then applied Luminol to the vinyl flooring in the kitchen. During this Luminol application, there was some reaction, giving an indication of a possible blood substance near the seam between the woodwork of the wall and the vinyl flooring, which was exactly the location that Zach described where the bodies were dragged out of the house.

Blood-stained wood trim between the kitchen steps and the laundry room. Stains were visible to the naked eye many months after the murders.

We removed that section of vinyl flooring as evidence and took several swabs of the subflooring, which was an old layer of vinyl flooring.

We then moved to the living room. We inspected the walls with the naked eye and then put Luminol on the walls in the specific areas where we thought blood spatter or cast off might be located and took swabs from the areas where we saw a positive reaction.

We took up the carpet and pad, which would have been the carpet installed by Rick Ginney. We applied Luminol to the floor areas pointed out by Johnny as having pools of blood when he went to clean the house, and where Zach described the bodies as located.

These areas too had positive reactions with the Luminol, so we decided the best way to preserve these areas would be to remove the entire section of wood flooring. We labeled each plank of oak flooring with numbers, photographed them in place, and then cut out the entire sections of floor with a saw. It was our idea to send the entire section of floor, piece by piece, to the DNA lab for testing.

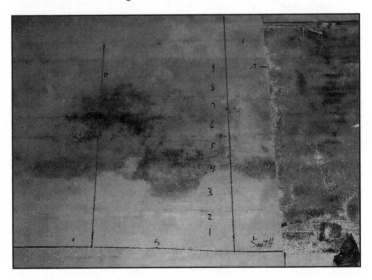

Oak flooring that had a positive reaction to Luminol, indicating blood. We cut out the section on the right and are preparing to cut the section on the left.

After two and a half days, we completed this process and had accumulated thirty-four pieces of evidence that included wood trim, linoleum pieces, swabs, and oak wood planking. This was as close to a television *CSI* production as I had ever seen, and Sonny Buvano should have been applauded for his efforts.

Bodies were dragged through this storage room, from the laundry room, out to the carport. Each marker indicates a potential blood stain on the path.

Now we had to take off our homicide detective hats and put on our interior decorator hats and put this house back together. Where did Roscoe and I go to buy new carpet and linoleum for this house? White's Carpet Mart. We picked out new flooring and convinced the owner of White's Carpet Mart to install it the next day, so we could start putting the furniture back in the house.

All in all, this process went off without a hitch. I figured this house now had the living room carpet replaced three times in the last two years.

We needed to compare some of the evidence taken from the house with the DNA of our victims. Having DNA comparisons done is not a cheap endeavor. By this time, I had established an account with the University of Nebraska Medical Center, which did DNA forensic testing for our department. Again, I contacted my FBI buddy who put up money to pay for this DNA research. This saved me having to deal with the chain of command approving the money costs.

By September 11, Sgt. Harry Bogowski, Roscoe, and I picked out four pieces of evidence from the house search that would most likely produce a DNA profile. This profile could then be compared with those of our victims, but the results—unlike the instant processing in the TV crime-scene labs—would not come back for at least six weeks. So we had to wait.

46
SOME GUILTY, PLEASE

The progression within the court system was still going on even though additional indictments had continued up until August.

Motions to Suppress Evidence were filed by the attorneys for Preston and Gaylan. The Motions to Suppress were based on the evidence gained in the twenty-four search warrants that had been served up to this point in the investigation, stating that the search warrants were not valid, thus the evidence should be suppressed.

The hearing lasted two days, September 19 and 20. The majority of the time during these hearings was spent on testimony of state's witnesses and entering the warrants and evidence seized into the court record. Finally, when the defense had the floor, they began to attack the warrants. They basically addressed one line in the affidavits, in which I described the relationship between Preston Blade and Gaylan Green as brothers, when they were actually cousins.

Because of this mischaracterization of the relationship, they argued all evidence should be seized and suppressed. Finally, on November 17, a sixty-seven-page ruling was issued by the federal court, denying all Motions to Suppress any evidence. Thank goodness my error didn't let a couple of murdering dope dealers go free.

Soon after this ruling, several of the indicted parties began to enter their guilty pleas. Chuck Nissan and Lavarius Blade entered guilty pleas, but did not cooperate and took their sentences straight up. Rick Ginney, Johnny Baustau, and Zach Woods pleaded guilty with cooperation agreements, but would not be sentenced until after the conclusion of the entire case. Yessica Tate tried to cooperate and had given a statement; however, she would not plead guilty and chose to go to trial and stand by her man.

47
LITTLE MAN
COMES CLEAN

While waiting for the results to come back from the University of Nebraska Medical Center's DNA testing lab, I stayed busy with mundane tasks, such as analyzing phone records on more than a dozen phones that had been identified as connected to several of the players in this investigation.

The goal was to verify contacts and relationships. It was early in the investigation that the red flag was raised on Rick Ginney, merely by his call frequency on one of Preston Blade's phones. These records were subpoenaed from the various phone companies, but it often takes months to receive the records back.

In the records request, you ask for a call detail report, which lists all the outgoing and incoming phone numbers. It was through these records that I would hand search line by line, trying to establish contacts between the different players. For example, if Preston had contact with any of the Arizona crew or if Preston or Gaylan had contact with any of the victims.

When the original subpoenas were sent out, I requested that the records be sent in two forms: formatted on a CD and the hard copies of the records. This was done for two reasons. In the computer formatted system, numbers could be downloaded in a computer program of all the phone numbers that were received, and the computer would search for common phone numbers. This was a much quicker way to do the research; however, it also depended on whether the information was correct on the computer files.

So as a backup, I made it my policy to do this research line by line, cross referencing the numbers by hand. By employing both methods, there was a higher level of assurance that the correct results would be found.

Even with the phones we had, I was aware that it was common practice for dope dealers, especially at this high level, to change their phones often and subscribe them in other people's names or use phone companies that are prepaid with flat rates that do not keep call detail records. So even with all this monotonous labor, our results could be fruitless.

While working on phone records in mid-October, I received a call from Zach Woods. At this time, Zach was on a release status prior to the trial for Preston, Gaylan, and Yessica. Again, this status of release was very uncomfortable for me because if anything happened to Zach, a key witness would be gone and the case would be damaged.

Not only did I worry about an actual hit—and I mean someone paid to kill him in regard to this case—but as a young gang member in the hood, his probability of getting killed over something stupid is very high.

"I'm pissed at you, man," Zach told me. Word was out on the street that Zach was "on the papers," which means that police reports had been released in discovery documents, identifying Zach and his statements that were made to the government.

"That's bullshit," I told Zach. "There's no way that your name is out because I haven't even put discovery out yet. Think about it. I would have nothing to gain by putting your name out there this soon. What probably is fucking happening is someone is putting stories out there trying to see how you're gonna react and they're trying to figure out if you're talking."

"Yah, that makes sense, man," he replied. "We need to get together. I need to clear some things up."

I had always felt he had left some items out, so I was eager to hear what this was all about. Arrangements were made to have Zach and his attorney meet with Lillian

Lomax, Roscoe, and me at the police station to clear up whatever it was.

This interview took place a few days later because with so many people involved and everyone's busy schedules, it was hard to coordinate a time when everyone could meet. That delay was worrisome to me because when I was on the phone with Zach, he was ready to talk and when you have a guy in the mood to talk, you jump on it. I just prayed that Zach was still in the talking mood when we finally met. He was.

Zach started by saying, "I want to clear something up. This is how it went."

I was paying close attention.

"When I arrive at the house next to the barber shop that night," he said, "it was earlier in the night, and when I get there it's Gaylan and three Mexican dudes."

"Give it to me from the beginning," I suggested, because I wanted to hear how the whole thing evolved with Shine and him.

Zach then began to talk chronologically about the beginning of his relationship with Preston. Zach began messing around with Shine since he was fifteen years old after meeting him on the block of Fortieth Avenue. Zach said while he was hanging out one day at the corner store, he was admiring a snake-skin belt Shine was wearing. Zach explained the school year was about to begin and Shine bought him a snake-skin belt as a gift and asked for nothing in return.

After about a year of seeing Shine on the block regularly and them having normal hello and goodbye interaction, Zach moved back to Texas where his mom lived. He returned to Omaha after a year, going right back to the Fortieth Avenue block, living with his grandmother and seeing Preston again. Zach said he was now going to high school and struggling for money, so Preston would buy him school clothes to help him out.

He started to get small bags of marijuana from Preston for personal use, but this quickly turned into Zach selling marijuana on the Fortieth Avenue block to customers who would drive through the neighborhood.

The Fortieth Avenue block was a busy open-air drug market for vehicles to just drive around the block until somebody would approach your car and ask what you wanted: crack, marijuana, pills. It was all available.

As Zach was selling more and more marijuana, his relationship with Preston grew stronger. Zach told us by January 2005, it was obvious that Preston had more and more money based on his lifestyle changes—lots of cars and always a big wad of money in his pocket.

That January Zach's own money got messed up with Preston because of a quantity of marijuana that was fronted to him—on the doper line of credit. But after this payment was made in full, the supply of marijuana that was being given to Zach went back to normal.

Zach then described how Preston and Gaylan started a music label business called Deuce's Down Music, and Zach was going to be a rapper for one of their groups, which was named Straight Dope. Zach said many CDs had been made of music that was recorded at two studios they were using; one was in the basement of the house on Fortieth Avenue, and the other was farther east in a real recording studio.

This information fit perfectly with evidence that had been recovered during the search warrants where we located about fifty CDs that had the name Straight Dope on them and several advertising posters for this rap group. The poster showed four young black guys, all being handcuffed by the police and on the ground. In front of the four guys was a duffel bag overflowing with money, and each of the bundles of money had a small black rubber band around it.

Ironically, some of the confiscated money in this case had small black rubber bands around thousand-dollar bundles of twenties, fifties, and hundreds. I speculated that the money in this poster was actually some of the money we recovered during the search warrants.

In March 2005, Preston talked about having something for Zach, which he believed was larger quantities of marijuana. During this conversation, Preston told Zach, "You'll have a lot of money soon." He was sure Zach would "be the only guy on the block with $500,000."

"About two or three days before the murders, I was riding with Preston, and he went to his stash house up south around Thirty-Seventh Street," Zach began the story about the actual murders. "There were two *esses* [a derogatory term for Hispanics] and a green car parked in front. I figured the car was theirs. But I didn't pay much attention cuz it had nothing to do with me. I just thought it was some drug deal going down.

"A couple days later, I got a call from a blocked number. It was Shine. He told me to come to the barber shop."

I asked him, "Is that unusual?"

"No, I would get calls to come all kinds of places just to kick it with him," he said. Zach called a jitney—an unlicensed taxi-like car and driver usually found in low-income areas. For a couple of bucks, the jitney dropped Zach at the barber shop.

When Zach arrived, he and Preston sat on the stoop in front of the barber shop for about ten or fifteen minutes, just kicking it and smoking a joint, talking about nothing really. They then walked to the house next door, which he knew was under the control of Preston.

"Once I go in the house, I about shit my pants. There are bales of weed stacked from floor to ceiling and the house is full. Barely any room to walk," Zach said.

Zach added there were also three "esses" in the house. "Two of them are the guys from the house up south," he said.

Preston told Zach, "Help the esses weigh all the weed."

Zach describes how he helped pick up each bale and put it on a large commercial scale. Weigh it. The oldest of the three Mexicans wrote each number down on a little piece of paper and used a calculator to add up the numbers. After all the bales were weighed, they were then moved into a U-Haul truck that was parked right next to the carport in the driveway.

Some of the bales were cut open and inspected for quality.

Zach said, "We did it so long. It took forever, like an hour and a half, man."

After all the marijuana was loaded into the truck, Preston and Gaylan left in the U-Haul, leaving him alone with the three Mexicans.

"I was taking to 'em. The biggest dude started bragging about how this was his operation, and he distributes marijuana all over. He said New York, Texas, Arkansas, and Pennsylvania."

While I'm talking with Zach, he told me he figured out the big guy and little guy were brothers. He continued to build credibility. He was there. His story was going to be right on.

After twenty minutes, Preston and Gaylan returned to the house with Gaylan walking to the kitchen and Preston standing in the hallway leading to the bedrooms, leaving the three Mexican guys in the living room, sitting on the couch.

Only seconds after Preston and Gaylan entered the house, Preston told Zach,

"Go outside and get my other phone out of the truck."

Zach said, "So I did what he said and went outside and walked to his truck that was parked in the driveway. As I'm getting up to the truck, I hear several pops."

"Do you mean gunshots?" I asked.

"Yah, gunshots. I know it's gunshots," he said. "I hear gunshots all the time. I live in the hood. I'm getting ready to run. I don't know who's shooting who. But before I can even get out of the driveway, Shine's at the front door and yelling at me, 'Get back up here.' "

As Zach reached the front porch, Gaylan and Preston were standing at the front door. Preston then told Gaylan to go back and take care of his business, at which time, Gaylan went back inside the house and Zach heard what he thought was one more gunshot.

Zach then stepped through the front door and described what he saw, "One of the esses was on the couch with his head against the wall and the other two were face down on the floor with large puddles of blood starting to run out around their heads."

Preston then started going off on him, "Take all the IDs and stuff off these guys." Before Preston and Gaylan left to take care of something, he told Zach, "If you don't do this, I'll make it look like you were the shooter."

Zach was in a state of shock. He didn't know what to do as he watched Preston and Gaylan get into Gaylan's black truck and start to drive toward the main street. Zach decided there was no way he was going to stay alone in the house with the three bodies, so he began to walk out the door heading toward the barber shop, but Preston saw him and yelled, "Get in the truck."

Zach told us he got in the truck and they drove to the stash house where he had been a couple days earlier where the two Mexicans had been seen. At this house, Preston pulled two guns from his waistband—one a revolver and one an automatic—and Gaylan pulled one gun from his waistband, and all these guns were hidden behind a bookcase at this house.

The three of them then drove to a gas station just a few blocks away, where Preston purchased gas in a small gas can. They then drove back to the house where the bodies were.

Gaylan backed into the driveway so the bed of the truck was closest to the house, and they went inside through the carport door, which led to the laundry room and kitchen. Once they were back inside the house, Preston went through the pockets of each of the three victims and took out their wallets and personal property and put them in a plastic bag.

At this point, Zach told us, "My hands were shaking. I was scared. Preston and Gaylan carried the two smaller guys out to the truck."

I said, "Tell me exactly the route they took."

Zach said, "They went through the living room, through the kitchen, down a couple steps, through the laundry room, into the carport, then into the truck. And the third guy was so big. They made me help."

Zach continued, "I had one leg, Gaylan had the other leg, and Preston had the shoulders, but even with all three of us, we dropped him in the kitchen and had to drag him the rest of the way."

After the bodies were loaded into the bed of the truck, they drove to the main street, just south of the house, went down to Sixtieth Street, then traveled north a long way to where there weren't any more houses and looked for a spot to drop the bodies. It was a wooded area and they pulled into a couple of driveways before finally backing into the final spot where the bodies were dumped.

Preston and Gaylan unloaded the bodies while Zach stood by the street as a lookout for any cars. Zach said after the bodies were out of the truck, he then saw a big fireball and heard a "whoosh" when they were lit on fire.

The three of them drove back to Preston's house on Fortieth Avenue and changed their clothes in the sloping backyard, off the secluded rutted alley that leads to the one-car garage that's part of the walkout basement. Preston took all the blood-covered clothes, doused them with gasoline and lit them on fire in a fire pit in the backyard.

Gaylan then realized he lost his phone. They were now worried that the phone was in the area where the bodies were just dumped and set on fire, but they were scared to go back there, so they decided to first check the house where the murders occurred. The phone was there. Gaylan was relieved that his phone was not at the site where the bodies were.

They then went back to the Fortieth Avenue block to Preston's house. At this time, Preston instructed Zach to go across the street to get Johnny Baustau to help clean up the murder scene. After Zach got Johnny, he walked to his grandmother's house, scared to death.

Several days after the murders, Zach said he saw Preston on Fortieth Avenue and they talked.

"Why didn't you just pay the dudes," Zach had asked Preston.

Preston responded in a very matter-of-fact way, "Any means necessary when dealing with money, I'm up $500,000 bucks, but this was about a couple million profit."

Zach's lengthy statement was detailed and included information that only someone with firsthand knowledge would know—details that were not public information. This included the piece of paper with the numbers written on it, the route the blood trail took at the dump scene, the relationship between the two brothers, the fact that the older Mexican only spoke Spanish, and the description of the green Pontiac G6 rented by Barry Willis.

In hindsight, I think Zach Woods only excluded one detail in this statement. From the autopsy, we knew that each victim had a mortal gunshot wound to the head. But John Doe 2 (Barry Willis) had two other gunshot wounds: one in his upper front shoulder and a second to his back shoulder.

I speculated that Zach was also forced by Shine to fire a round into one of the bodies so he would be implicated if the cops ever got close. This theory seemed logical, but Zach didn't come that far and I guess I don't blame him.

As Zach was giving his statement, I experienced a feeling only a few other cops ever approach: your attention is at its peak, you are processing every word being spoken and comparing each word against case facts known only to you—and those who had committed the crimes. As these factors square up with each other, you are hearing firsthand about the murders you've been spending night and day, month after month to track down the killers. You actually get chills as details unfold.

This kind of interaction doesn't happen very often. But when it does …

To put this into perspective, I have been an undercover officer on multi-pound purchases of cocaine with tens of thousands of dollars involved, and the bad guy getting arrested right in front of me is intense stuff. But it doesn't even factor on the scale when compared to a confession regarding involvement in a murder. This is what Zach Woods just did.

48
UPPING THE ANTE

On the 5th of December, I received an early Christmas and Hanukkah present from Melissa of the Human DNA Identification Laboratory at the University of Nebraska Medical Center. Melissa said that the numbers were in for the four pieces of evidence submitted. They had extremely high numbers of probability that the blood from these samples came from John Doe 3, Floreno Gonzalez.

DNA is sometimes confusing. In reality, they don't say it is a match, they say what the probability is. In this case, the report read that the probability of an unrelated individual matching the DNA profiles from the specimens, given that Floreno Gonzalez expresses this DNA profile, is 1 in 900 quintillion (that's 10 to the 18th power) for Caucasians, 1 in 91.76 sextillion (that's 10 to the 21st power) for African Americans, and 1 in 323 quintillion (that's 10 to the 18th power) for Hispanic Americans.

So based on the number of people in the world's population being greatly smaller than these numbers, in all reality, it is a match. This information was quickly relayed to Lillian Lomax of the U.S. Attorney's office and Georgeann Goldstein of the County Attorney's office.

Holy moley! We got it! Let's file some murder charges!

Within days, Roscoe and I did a process called paper booking, which means to book a suspect on charges when the suspect is already in custody on unrelated charges, then providing the suspects with their booking sheets.

Who knows? Maybe Preston and Gaylan would confess when we give them these papers. I seriously doubted it, but knew it would be fun to see the "I stepped in shit" look on their faces. However, the entire time, Roscoe and I planned on maintaining a very professional and matter-of-fact demeanor.

The ante in this game had gotten higher. It was determined that the federal conspiracy case would be concluded before the murder trial would ever start in court. Just to add fuel to the fire, Georgeann Goldstein filed the paperwork after the murder charges were filed, enhancing this prosecution to a death penalty prosecution. This booking led to the third wave of media attention in this case. The only thing left was to have a trial so the media could hear all the gory details.

I must have been a good boy that year because I got another Hanukkah and Christmas present early. Lilly Lomax called me and told me she had found an obscure federal sentencing guideline regarding enhancements on conspiracy cases, which in simpler terms means that during the conspiracy, if the death of another person is caused, the enhancement is punishable by up to life in prison.

So Lilly amended the charges to include this enhancement with the hefty potential sentence of life imprisonment just on the federal conspiracy charges, before we even got to the state murder charges.

This case had the makings for one whale of a trial. It would definitely be a public spectacle. The clock was ticking and it was time to get ready for trial, when all of a sudden the whole process came to a screeching halt.

Gaylan's attorney received a judgeship in county court, so a new attorney needed to be appointed and given adequate time to learn the case. By this time, nearly all the discovery had been turned over to defense, except for a few of the key reports regarding testifying witnesses, which would be turned over just prior to trial.

When Preston's attorney heard this news, he quickly seized this window of opportunity and claimed a personal conflict based on the new timetable for the trial to take place and was also excused from the case. So now we needed two new attorneys and the entire process was put on hold.

It is my belief that the waiting process definitely goes to the advantage of the defense merely because the longer the time between the trial and the actual crimes, the worse witnesses' memories become, witnesses can die or not be found, or witnesses can become intimidated. Plenty of variables worked against the prosecution by these delays. But there was nothing we could do about it.

49
GOOD LAWYER, BAD LAWYER

As we waited to see who the court would now appoint to represent Preston and Gaylan, I was just praying it would be two good defense attorneys.

That may seem odd to hear coming from a cop, but my consideration and evaluation of a lawyer being described as a good one comes at many levels.

First and foremost is obviously the skill level of the counsel for the defendant. I do not want some loser doing a bad job that could open up the possibilities of an appeal down the road for inadequate counsel.

Second, it would be nice to get attorneys who are cordial and decent to have contact with. What I mean by this is some defense lawyers want to make everything a federal case (pun intended), and they act as if their client was an angel and the cops have done all these devious things to trap their client.

I really don't know how some defense lawyers do it because, at some point, they have to look at the evidence and know their client did it, whatever the case is— whether it's murder or jaywalking. With that said, if the defendant is innocent of a crime, I absolutely believe in the judicial system and the right to defend yourself.

The range of defense lawyer types is wide. I had a defense lawyer go into a tirade in front of a jury because I was not giving the answer he wanted. He kept repeating the same question over and over, actually addressing the judge saying, "He is not giving me the answer I want."

The whole time I was just waiting for the prosecutor to object, but no objections came. Finally I responded to the defense lawyer by telling him, "It's my answer, not yours, you can't dictate my thought process."

Later I asked the prosecutor Georgeann Goldstein why there were no objections when the defense lawyer was going off on me on the stand. The prosecutor calmly replied, "The defense lawyer was looking like an asshole in front of the jury, and I didn't want to stop him." I thought that made sense.

Sometimes it gets petty with defense lawyers, misstating facts within their questions and trying to catch you making a mistake by agreeing with their misrepresentation. Usually they are talking quickly when they try this, so all you do is slow them down and ask them to repeat the question or ask them to review your reports and then point out their inaccuracies.

Then the defense lawyer will politely say thank you for pointing that out. But if you had agreed with the misstatement, look out. Quickly, you can be made to look like the most stupid cop who doesn't know any of the actual facts of the case.

This pettiness can really get low. I have had defense lawyers mispronounce and butcher my name, I believe, in an attempt to distract me from my testimony. But that can be a two-way street. I was getting badgered by a defense lawyer once whose name when said quickly sounded like "nut lick." So that's exactly how I addressed him: Mr. Nutlick. I've often wondered how the court reporter put that in the transcripts.

But getting back to why defense lawyers do the job they do. There is one other reason that comes to mind other than for the noble idea that every person deserves a good defense—and that simply is money.

When I was an undercover narcotics cop, on many occasions after the suspect was arrested and had a couple of hearings in the court system, such as the preliminary hearing in state court, the U.S. Attorney's office would adopt the case. There would be an initial appearance in federal court, followed by a detention hearing, and then the suspect would want to cooperate and give a proffer interview.

During this process, the suspect would call me and complain about how he had paid his lawyer $25,000, but now after the second hearing, the lawyer wanted more money because he had used up the $25,000 already in fees. In my mind, I was laughing about the suspect getting screwed, but then I was also pissed because I didn't find this extra quantity of money during my investigation.

Ultimately, this defense lawyer would go to the judge and pull out of the case, saying that the client does not have adequate funds to pay his fees. Then what generally happens is this: the defense lawyer goes to the judge who excuses the lawyer from the case and appoints a public defender or a private defense lawyer, who is then paid a standard rate—fees that are paid by us taxpayers.

Even with all these negative defense lawyer stories, I must admit there are good ones. I have developed professional relationships with many of them, which works out well, especially when the defense lawyer calls me when a guy wants to cooperate.

Soon, the new defense lawyers were named for Preston and Gaylan. Both new lawyers were solid and had good reputations: one of whom I had come up against in a prior murder case and the other I had never had personal interaction with, but heard he would try to antagonize the witnesses. I thought we would surely have plenty of witnesses for him to antagonize.

These two new defense lawyers had volumes of data to process, so the trial was still months away.

50
WAITING FOR TRIAL

Waiting for trial to begin, I got back into a normal rotation of taking new cases, mostly felony assaults and assisting in the primary investigations of new murder cases. No murder cases were assigned to me.

Some follow-up was still taking place, shoring up loose ends on different interviews. I had extreme anxiety during this time because Johnny Baustau, Zach Woods, and Rick Ginney were all still on release status, and I feared something bad could happen to one or all of them.

Lilly Lomax proposed that we get them in custody to start serving their time early even though they had not been sentenced yet, then that time could be applied to their sentences. This was a great idea, but telling and selling this to each of them was going to be like asking them to eat a shit sandwich. We actually pulled it off.

Between each of their attorneys and Lilly's charm, at least these three witnesses were placed in a controlled and protected environment. Other witnesses who were being housed in other facilities throughout the United States, such as Kenny Boston, who was in Phoenix, and Eli Martinez, who was in Texas, were being brought back to Omaha and housed in local facilities until the trial.

Wilson Mack was still out on bond regarding his hog-tie bandit robberies. When I tried to convince him to chill out in jail for a couple of months, he was fit to be tied and said no way. I had no leverage on him, so we let it go, just hoping he didn't get killed or in trouble in the meantime.

Montel Jones—the linchpin in our early investigation and the first to name Shine—had already been murdered in an unrelated incident, so we had lost him as a witness. But the original police report from the incident when he was shot by Shine listed his sister as a witness to the event, but there were no reports regarding any interviews with her. Roscoe and I talked to her in an attempt to get a statement.

Montel's sister, Shameka Jones, was a petite, quiet, mild-mannered young lady. She not only witnessed the shooting, but she spoke to Preston before the shooting when he knocked on the door looking for Montel, telling her he was Shine and to tell Montel he was looking for him.

After she had the conversation with Shine, she watched as he walked back across the street and sat in a maroon Monte Carlo on the passenger side with another black man sitting in the driver's seat.

Shameka said a few minutes later she heard a commotion outside and went to the door to see what it was. She saw Montel struggling with Shine who had a gun out and was trying to force Montel inside the car. As Montel struggled with Shine, the gun went off and hit Montel in the leg.

At that point, Shine got in the car with the driver, and they drove away. Shameka was shown a photo lineup of both Preston and Gaylan, but could not pick either out of the lineups.

When asked if she would testify regarding this incident, Shameka was reluctant and scared, saying it was not any of her business, but she would think about it and talk to her mother and let us know.

Things were also beginning to change in the homicide unit during this waiting period. Roscoe had an opportunity to leave homicide and go back to the narcotics unit, which he did, but he still had the ability to work with me on clean-up matters in this case. The homicide unit Lieutenant N.S. Boss was getting promoted to Captain, and Sgt. Harry Bogowski was planning to retire.

I could see the writing on the wall. I should also try to get out while the getting was good. Survival in the police department can be hard. I'm not talking about street survival. I'm talking about internal, political bullshit survival. The best thing you can do, especially if an officer wants to do real police work, is find a unit with a command staff, specifically a lieutenant and sergeant, with that same thought process.

Unfortunately, this is not an easy thing to do. I believe over time the promotional process in law enforcement has somehow taken the edge off crime fighting and put a bigger emphasis on looking good in the public eye and not pissing anybody off. More people are thinking about promotions than about putting bad guys in jail.

The promotional process begins with a test of the Standard Operating Procedures and some knowledge of laws. That's fair enough, except there are always people who actually fail this written test who are moved on to the next step of the promotional process because of consent decrees for race and gender.

The next step is the assessment center, which is a mock exercise consisting of a written response to a few questions, a videotaped subordinate interview with a role player, which is graded by outside assessors, and an "inbox" assessment. This inbox assessment is the practice of handling whatever issues are in your packet, simulating a supervisor's normal daily emails and correspondence.

Companies actually travel across the country to cities prior to promotional testing, teaching officers how to perform these tasks and the subordinate interview. Specifically, the goal of the inbox is to address all issues presented, not solve them. This process creates a mindset of passing problems on to others because once it is off your desk, it is no longer a problem to you.

The task is really more of a game than anything else. However, when applied in the real world, this mindset produces a situation where some command officers spend more time trying to figure who they can pass off a problem or issue to than just trying to solve it in the first place.

I have seen this take place in the real world. A citizen complaint gets passed around to four or five different sergeants, ending up with the sergeant it was originally given to, just because of this "let somebody else do it" mindset.

The worst thing about the promotional process is there is no calculation of an officer's past performance either to lower or raise his or her ranking. It is common for an officer with a history of foolishness, laziness, or straight stupidity in the real world—regarding probable cause, search and seizure, and general police work—to rank somewhere on a promotional list and still get promoted.

It is a shame a chief doesn't have some viable veto power in these situations. I guess I don't blame the chief though. If he had to stand up in this way and damage an applicant, it would surely lead to a lawsuit.

Oh, well. These issues are beyond my control, so you just roll with it and try to control your own environment, looking for command that is smart and driven by the simple idea that good police work puts the bad guys in jail.

I was looking for a new job and now Captain N.S. Boss hooked me up with an FBI Task Force focusing on gang violence and drugs, which sounded good.

So when I met with my new sergeant at this new job, I described the triple murder investigation and gave notice of the likely four- to six-week upcoming trial and probably the need for two weeks for preparation prior to the trial.

During this two-hour briefing, this sergeant just looked at me like a deer in the headlights and said, "Okay." It was as if the two-hour story just went over her head.

In hindsight, I later wondered if maybe the entire case, when represented to somebody, was overwhelming and this sergeant was just caught off guard by the complexity and size of the case.

51
FINAL PREP FOR JUSTICE

The trial date was set for the middle of October 2007—two and a half years after the bodies were found burning—with five weeks blocked out on the judge's calendar for the trial to run its course. I thought this was good timing because the trial would be over before the holidays.

Even though Yessica Tate had given a proffer statement to the government, she could not turn on her man, Preston, and testify against him. Instead she was going to trial, sitting at the defense table next to Preston and Gaylan. This was quite a gamble for the young mother of two. With cooperation she may have faced a minimal sentence; however, by going to trial, she could face many more years in prison.

The defense attorney who represented Yessica attempted to have her trial separated from Preston and Gaylan's, citing that the actions of those two would cast negative light on Yessica during the trial if all were tied together. My feelings on this were, *No shit.* But let's be realistic: they were all part of the same conspiracy so they all should be held at the same time.

The judge agreed with me. The trial was kept as one case, setting the stage for a courtroom that would have three defense tables and a detailed security plan designed by the U.S. Marshals Service, calling for deputies to be brought in from across the country to man all the duties.

A special courtroom in the federal courthouse designated for Supreme Court hearings in this district had to be used because the overall size of this courtroom was large enough. It could handle the area for all the defense tables and had a sizable gallery for the anticipated crowds.

In the weeks prior to the trial, orders had been placed transporting our incarcerated witnesses back to Omaha to be housed in jails in the surrounding area. When Eli Martinez, who was the load driver, finally arrived from federal prison in Texas, a court order transferring him into our custody was completed. The last time we spoke to Eli, he could not identify the house where he delivered the load of marijuana from photos of the houses that I had shown him. I wanted him to check and see if the yellow house where the murders transpired was the same house where the load was delivered, since the description he had previously given was exactly the same.

We randomly drove by four or five houses, asking him if it was the one, and Martinez continually gave a negative response. We then drove by the area of Lincoln Coolidge's house. Before we even got on the block, Martinez said, "This looks familiar." Then as we pulled in front of the yellow house, Martinez was in disbelief, stating, "I can't believe it. That's it right there; 100 percent, that's the house."

The potential witness list compiled by Lilly Lomax was nearing over a hundred people, ranging from custodians of records of banks, airlines, rental companies, and cell phone companies, to pathologists, DNA experts, jewelry experts and appraisers, accountants, crime laboratory technicians, and over thirty police officers, in addition to all the co-conspirators, who would be called to testify.

Each of these people would need to be contacted to review their statements and obtain current contact information for them so we could give them an estimate of when they would testify, so their personal schedules would not be completely inconvenienced by keeping them on hold for the entire five-week period.

There's an old saying that the best way for a woman to win a man's heart is through his stomach. As I think about my own life and love of food, it certainly made sense to me. Now, let me expand on that theory. The best way to solidify an incarcerated, testifying co-conspirator is also through his stomach.

At some point during my career, I started feeding a nice restaurant meal to these guys during their pretrial meeting with us at the U.S. Attorney's office. It started innocently enough one time after I picked up a guy at the county jail to transport over to the U.S. Attorney's office.

I was really hungry, so I hit a drive-through hamburger joint. I didn't want to be rude, so I asked the inmate if he wanted anything and, of course, he said yes. The guy couldn't believe I bought him something to eat. He was so grateful to me after all those jailhouse meals. So, here we sat, me and the inmate, breaking bread and talking about sports, girls, and general B.S.

As this tradition evolved over my career, it revolved around my three favorite restaurants. My first favorite place is Jim's Rib Haven, a BBQ joint owned by an ex-Marine from Mississippi. His smoked meat is the best I've ever had. He still smokes a turkey for me every Thanksgiving.

My next food paradise is King Kong's, a gyro shop owned by an immigrant named Nick, whose accent is strong and his portions even stronger. Nick's a perfect double for John Belushi yelling, "Chee-burger, chee-burger, chips. Coke, no Pepsi." He serves a triple Kong burger that weighs one and a half pounds.

Last, but certainly not least, is Julio's Tex Mex restaurant. I actually took Eli Martinez there after our house drive-bys. He said the Mexican food was delicious, but even more importantly, he said it was authentic. My passion at Julio's though is the mushroom burger, which is covered with a secret sauce called "gringo sauce." This thing just melts in your mouth.

Food may not seem like a big deal, but this gesture of eating with these guys as an equal definitely creates bonds that minimize the worry that one of them would get cold feet at the last second and not testify. Let's not forget reality that people do get killed over this kind of stuff.

Lilly Lomax had obtained a secured storage room, approximately fifteen feet by fifteen feet, in the basement of the federal courthouse in the federal grand jury area. This would be the location where we kept all the evidence prior to admitting it during the trial. Not all of the 500-plus pieces of evidence booked into the police department's property room were going to be used, but well over 250 of them would be.

Roscoe and I had to sign out each item into our custody and then transport it to the federal courthouse where it would remain until the conclusion of the trial. This process literally took days. The final result: all the evidence, and most impressively all those bales of marijuana, completely filled this storage room.

One thing we did not anticipate was how foul the smell would become from the marijuana. The entire basement of the federal courthouse began to reek of marijuana.

In federal court, the government can designate a case officer to sit at the prosecution table, even if this person testifies during the trial. Lilly Lomax informed me I would do this task.

My testimony during the case would not occur during one sitting, but she would continually recall me throughout the entire trial, describing each step of the investigation as it occurred. Based on this assignment, I now had to not only get all the witnesses ready with Lilly, but I had to get myself ready, so reading all reports was filling any of my spare time at night.

As Lilly was getting all the witnesses lined up, she was also getting her opening statement prepared. In doing this, she would give a brief description of the entire case. Lilly told me she was rehearsing this at home in the evenings. Even though the opening statement was a brief overview of the entire case, it took her over two hours to get through it.

Lilly then described to me how she got her creative mojo going and actually incorporated the home video we located of Preston and Gaylan counting the money with the marijuana on the table in front of them, which would be displayed on a huge screen in front of the jury box.

I was getting anxious to get this thing going. As good as this case was, the whole process starts to get old. After a while it takes its toll on your life outside of the job: I missed kids' softball games or I'd take my recorder to games, sit on the bleachers, and dictate supplemental reports. My family was often detoured with me as I checked a surveillance spot. I was preparing witnesses and preparing myself for testimony.

It's all I had thought about for two years. I was ready for this case to be closed.

52
THE BIG SHOW

Trial day had finally come. The judicial process had reached its apex. All of the pretrial hearings and motions were completed, having paved the path to the top of the justice mountain.

Our case would be presented to an impartial jury to decide the guilt or innocence of the three defendants. Even though this case had a primary foundation evolving from a drug conspiracy, it would also be presented just like a murder trial because of the enhancement regarding the conspiracy, because the death of another person resulting from the conspiracy can lead to an enhancement of life in prison. However, before the actual trial started, we needed a jury.

The first morning of the trial, I sensed the tension in the air. It was coming from everywhere. The defense attorneys were organizing their tables and carts of paperwork, and the Marshals were checking the security plan, which included a metal detector outside of the courtroom, in addition to an ID check of each spectator entering the courtroom. This was a very key aspect of the Marshals' security plan because within the first two or three days, several potential spectators were arrested on outstanding warrants prior to even getting in the courtroom.

Word of this scrutiny spread like wildfire on the streets, which minimized the representation of supporting thug gang members who wanted to come to the trial. These types of people in the courtroom really didn't matter that much to me, but think if you were Zach Woods, Johnny Baustau, or Rick Ginney, and one of these thugs from the gang is staring you down as you testify. We already knew from way back in this investigation during the monitoring of jail calls that intimidation of witnesses was one tactic that Preston had tried to employ.

I sat at the prosecution table facing the judge's bench. The prosecution was positioned to the judge's left closest to the jury box, with two tables behind it, balancing out the room with the three defense tables to the judge's right. These remaining two tables behind the prosecution's table were used to house paperwork and a station for the audio/visual magician from the U.S. Attorney's office, who would operate any displays on the large screen controlled by a computer.

Lilly Lomax sat closest to the defense tables. A second attorney was assigned to assist Lilly, who sat in the middle, and I sat directly next to the jury box, literally five feet away from the jurors. The jurors were situated in a two-tiered jury box, sitting in padded leather swivel chairs.

As spectators began to fill the courtroom, I recognized family members of each defendant. It definitely did not look like a united front in the gallery either. Each family was sitting in their own little section, which made sense.

Yessica's mother was pissed at Preston Blade for getting her into this whole mess. Gaylan's family was pissed at Preston because at one point he tried to put the murder on Gaylan during his proffer, and in the recorded jail calls, Preston talked about having witnesses say it was all Gaylan's doing. Gaylan's family definitely showed up in the largest numbers and most regularly.

One thing that certainly caught my eye was not only the large number of female family members Gaylan had, but how nicely they were dressed. These women, specifically Gaylan's mother, had beautiful dresses, and they looked expensive. I never saw any of his women in the same dress twice.

To put that into perspective, I was trying to figure out a rotation of my five suits and ten neckties, so the jury wouldn't figure out how often I was wearing the same clothes.

The defendants were transported by the U.S. Marshal Service in an unmarked van every day from the county correctional center to the federal courthouse, where they were changed from their orange jumpsuits into street clothes. They were escorted into the courtroom with no handcuffs or shackles for the jury to see, preventing any subconscious negative opinion about the defendants to be construed by the jury.

But under their clothing, the defendants were wearing a stun belt with a U.S. Marshal assigned to the trigger of each belt. The Marshal was ready to activate this belt by remote control if a security breach would occur. An electrical jolt would drop the defendant like a log.

The courtroom had filled and the trial was ready to begin. The bailiff called the court to order, and all parties rose as the federal judge entered the courtroom from a hidden door in the wall behind the judge's bench.

As we settled into our chairs, she addressed the court and greeted all parties of significance, specifically each defendant and their attorneys and the prosecutor. As usual, somebody from the gallery would shout words of support to one of the defendants.

Usually the judge would give one admonishment regarding gallery conduct, but from that point on, the U.S. Marshals removed any person causing any disruption in the courtroom and banned them from returning. Within the first day, a couple of people had to be tossed, setting the tone for a smooth trial without disruption or distraction.

The judge then gave a progression outline for the trial with an opportunity for each attorney to raise any questions. All interactions and statements were documented by the court reporter, who sat in front of a computer in a chair just below the level of the judge's bench. The first item in the progression of the trial was to select a jury. The jury is picked from a pool of potential jurors that are summoned to the courthouse for jury duty based on voter registration.

From this pool, thirty-four people were selected randomly to report to our courtroom as potential jurors in this case. This number was much higher than normal because in this case, during the voir dire process, all three defense attorneys had the power to strike or remove a potential juror, and so could the prosecutor, until the pool is down to twelve jurors and two alternates, who would be the jurors who actually hear the case.

Once the jury was selected, the next order of business was the presentation of opening statements. Each attorney had an opportunity to address the jury. The prosecution gave a preview of the evidence that would be presented and how the evidence supported the indicted charges, and an evaluation of this evidence would lead the jury to have a finding of guilt.

Just to the contrary, the defense would try to explain how there is no evidence to lead to any findings of guilt, only a finding of not guilty.

Lilly Lomax was born to be a courtroom lawyer. Her presence in the courtroom was perfect. Her walk was confident and tall, and she had a never-ending sophisticated wardrobe of business suits and dresses. As she walked in front of the jurors making her opening statements, all eyes were fixed on her and everyone listened to her every word. Her delivery was flawless during the two-hour oral address. Lilly had definitely set the bar high for the defense attorneys to follow.

In the preparation of the opening statement, Lilly had originally planned to play the home video that showed Gaylan counting money and Preston as the cameraman. But just before the opening statements, Lilly decided not to use it, fearing that its presentation prior to its admission into evidence could be troublesome later.

The courtroom is like a battlefield, and the attorney must make decisions (some very quickly) whether to be aggressive or conservative, to attack or wait for a more opportune time to attack. Lilly also possessed this important quality.

It took until nearly the end of the second full day for all of the opening statements to be completed. The next phase was the presentation of the prosecution's case. The presentation took the same course as the actual investigation by traveling in two directions on a timeline. The starting point was to be the morning the three burning bodies were discovered.

With this starting point, witnesses that were called included the first responding officer who found the bodies. This was followed up by the scene investigator, Isadore Demann. During Isadore's testimony, the crime scene, the location of the bodies, and the surrounding area was described. This description also included the blood trails on the street nearly a half-mile in each direction near where the bodies were dumped.

Isadore also described the recovery of the two items off the bodies located in the pants pockets: the hotel receipt in the pocket of Barry Willis and the small piece of paper with the six columns of numbers located in the pants pocket of Floreno Gonzalez.

The pathologist then testified as to the cause of death determined through the autopsy. During this testimony, the gunshot wounds to the victims were described and cited as the cause of death. The pathologist also explained how the burn markings on the bodies were post-death damage, based on the lack of soot and smoke residue in the lungs or airways.

After the prosecution finished the direct testimony of each witness, each of the three defense attorneys had an opportunity to ask questions during cross-examination. The prosecutor could then ask questions of the witness in what is called redirect. Finally, the defense has the last opportunity in recross to ask any questions that arose from the previous volley of questioning.

This process takes place for every witness. Obviously, some witnesses have more involved roles than others, so the length of time any one witness is on the stand can vary greatly.

I was called to the stand next for the first of many times throughout this trial and detailed my initial involvement in the investigation, which included the canvassing of the crime scene and the assignment of victimology, or researching the victims. I described how my investigation began by a simple follow-up on the hotel receipt, leading to several trips to Phoenix, Arizona, which then led to the information regarding narcotics activity between the victims and two black males from Omaha named "Shine" and "Nephew."

This personal testimony also described our inability to identify either of those two nicknames until information came to light months later from the felony assault investigation conducted by Detective Zachary George.

Detective George then testified, describing his felony assault victim named Montel Jones, who named his assailants as "Shine," real name Preston Blade, and "Nephew," real name Gaylan Green.

Unfortunately, Montel was now dead and could not be called as the next logical witness. We still had Montel's sister Shameka Jones, but she was reluctant to be involved in this trial. To protect our interests, a material witness warrant was written for both Shameka and the follow-up witness to her, Wilson Mack, who had the gun battle with Shine and Nephew.

I had never been involved with a material witness arrest before. I think I had only heard about one on television up to that point in my life. As Roscoe and I were driving to Shameka's house, I was trying to predict what her reaction would be to this arrest, and my thoughts were not positive. This all came after a full day in the courtroom.

We found Shameka right away at home and advised her of the situation. We promised her she would be the first witness called in the morning, and we would take her back home right after she testifies. I really felt bad about it, but it had to be done for the greater good. If I had to do it all over again, maybe I would have tried to get a hotel room and guard it all night, but I'm sure an idea like that would have created all kinds of issues with police command for overtime and the hotel bill.

After securing Shameka into jail, Roscoe and I then went on the hunt for Wilson Mack, whom we coaxed to meet us with a phone call. He was most certainly pissed off, and his attitude made me not feel all that bad about his night spent in jail. But I hoped he would get over it before he had to testify the next morning.

True to our word, Shameka was the first to testify the next morning, and we had her home before noon. As it turned out, she was probably even a better witness than her brother would have been if he was alive. It's kind of strange the way that turned out.

I then took the stand again, explaining how Wilson Mack was the hog-tie bandit and how he was connected to this investigation. The stage was set and Wilson took center stage.

I was on the edge of my seat, just waiting to see what his demeanor was going to be. He took the stand and was articulate in a straightforward, street kind of way that I think the jury actually liked. During the cross-examination, one of the defense attorneys was really trying to discredit Wilson with his criminal history and pending cases.

Wilson calmly replied to this defense attorney, "I'm a jacker. That's what I do. I'm not hiding anything." A *jacker* is a street term for someone who is a robber. All in all, we got through one of our biggest wild cards and things were going well.

Now that we had established that the nickname Shine was Preston Blade and the nickname Nephew was Gaylan Green, the trial changed directions on the timeline, actually traveling back in time regarding the historical research on Preston "Shine" Blade and Gaylan "Nephew" Green.

I again took the stand and described the research portion of our case. This portion of the trial was a constant parade of dozens of witnesses detailing each real estate purchase, each vehicle purchase, police officers from past law enforcement contacts, such as the airport interdiction stop with $47,000 being located on Preston, the drunk driving arrest of Preston just after the murders with $12,000, and the speeding incident with Gaylan having a pound of marijuana and nearly $10,000.

Representatives were called from the major airlines, including Delta, Southwest, Continental, America West, and Northwest Airlines, documenting flight records for Preston and Gaylan between Omaha and Phoenix. Representatives from cell phone companies were called to explain cell phone records that documented contacts among the specific individuals within this conspiracy.

Most memorable of this phase of witnesses was the accountant who worked for a very reputable accounting firm and completed both Preston's and Gaylan's previous year's tax returns, which listed their occupations as a lawn service business and personal services business. On this tax return, they each reported an income of $225,000, with each party paying approximately $30,000 in federal taxes.

Lilly Lomax had this accountant on the witness stand and asked him questions about the tax returns and the documentation provided by Preston and Gaylan so he could complete the tax filings. It was just wonderful watching this guy twist and readjust himself on the witness stand. He was literally squirming. Eventually, he admitted that there was no documentation. He testified that he just plugged in "industry standards."

I'm thinking to myself, *What the heck are industry standards for personal services? I think there should be an a/k/a next to personal services saying drug dealer.* Lilly was definitely on the offensive with this guy. And what was even funnier about the whole situation is he was called as our witness.

The next portion of the trial changed the timeline. Instead of going back in time, we moved forward in the investigation, with the preparation and execution of all the search warrants. Officers from each search warrant team were called as witnesses to explain items recovered from each warrant and entered as evidence. This was where the bulk of the marijuana, the large sums of money, the handguns, the rifle, and numerous vehicles were all entered into the court record.

By the end of the trial, over 760 pieces of evidence were entered for the jury to consider.

It was also during this phase that the video from the camcorder recovered from the search warrant at Yessica's apartment was played. The jury watched and listened as Preston and Gaylan boasted of their successful business, displaying the money, cars, and marijuana. The courtroom was dead still. Not only was the jury transfixed on the large screens, but so was the gallery. This was definitely a major blow to the defense.

Another strategy employed at this stage of the trial— and visually impressive—was the display of all the marijuana recovered from the warrants.

Roscoe and I used carts and hauled up all the marijuana during the lunch break and stacked the bales of marijuana three high, basically building a wall around the jury box, so when court resumed, this immense wall of marijuana bales was just out of their reach. It is one thing to talk about the marijuana, but once physically seen, the enormity of the seizure puts it in a context that is nearly overwhelming.

Roscoe and I had to take the marijuana back to the storage room each night for security purposes. After the second or third day of the marijuana being brought to the trial, the courtroom began to smell, so the judge ordered that it be removed and left out of the courtroom for the remainder of the trial. Each bale or small baggie of marijuana had to be tested by a forensic lab to verify that it was in fact a controlled substance. Two technicians from the forensic lab testified to each piece of evidence being submitted for testing as to the results—sure enough, it was marijuana.

This then led to the jail phone call review. During this phase, ten calls were played and entered into evidence. It was through these calls that information began to be developed regarding Rick Ginney, Johnny Baustau, Zach Woods, and Lincoln Coolidge. After these correlations were established, the testimony of these individuals began.

Lincoln Coolidge's testimony, simply enough, put the control of the murder scene in the hands of his distant cousin, Preston, who had the barber shop next door.

The testimony of Rick Ginney described his role in the transportation of marijuana from Phoenix to Omaha and the transportation of money from Omaha to Arizona after the airport interdiction. His testimony also included when he recarpeted the house next to the barber shop and melted the handguns for Preston.

Johnny Baustau was up next and testified about his cleanup of the blood at the house next to the barber shop at the request of Preston and how he witnessed the removal of the couch and carpet by Preston and Gaylan from that same house where the blood was located. We never found where the couch and carpet were dumped.

Last, as clean-up batter, was Zach Woods, who placed the victims at the house next to the barber shop on the night of the murders and observed the house full of marijuana, with our prime suspects, Preston and Gaylan, being present. Zach then described the weighing process of the marijuana, with the oldest Mexican writing down numbers and using a calculator. Zach talked about how they loaded the marijuana into the U-Haul truck and how Preston and Gaylan left for a period of time before returning in Gaylan's black Chevy Silverado truck.

Zach finally explained how, after Preston and Gaylan returned, they entered the residence and sent him outside to retrieve the cell phone from the truck. Zach testified how only after a few seconds outside, he heard gunshots being fired from inside the house and Preston appeared at the doorway and told Zach not to leave. Zach also testified how Gaylan appeared at the door and Preston told Gaylan to "take care of his" and how Gaylan went back inside and Zach heard another gunshot.

Zach then described how he saw the aftermath of the three dead bodies and how the removal of the bodies transpired, with them being dumped in a wooded area and set on fire. Zach talked about how they returned to Preston's house on Fortieth Avenue, where he was instructed to get Johnny Baustau. This all correlated with Johnny's testimony.

Zach's testimony then led to the forensic search of the house next to the barber shop, Lincoln Coolidge's house. I again testified about the permission to search this property and the search and recovery of evidence, which appeared to be blood, and how it was sent for DNA testing and comparison to our victims with positive results.

The DNA expert witnesses then testified to the process of the comparisons and gave the statistical results that they matched the victims. This ended the prosecution's case.

The defense had an opportunity to call its witnesses. We had been going for nearly four and a half weeks. Among all three defendants, only two witnesses were called: Yessica's mother and grandmother who basically said she was a good girl.

It was now time for closing arguments. Lilly Lomax again did a complete overview of the case, citing witnesses' testimonies and corroborating physical evidence that supported each party's testimony. The defense closed with attempts to discredit our case in lieu of any case they made on their own.

A break was needed before the jury would be read its instructions from the judge prior to going into deliberations. It was late in the day. This process would all begin the following morning.

53
TO THE JURY

The next day I felt relaxed in the courtroom. My job was now done. The judge spent nearly the entire morning reading the jury instructions on how the jury was to process the evidence and make their finding on each of the counts in the indictments.

These instructions are a very important part of the legal process. If the judge does not provide the jurors with these instructions, then the defense could later appeal any verdict that results.

For me, it was a morning to just sit back and think of the entire process. The feeling, hunch, or maybe even theory that I had been developing throughout the trial and even earlier in this investigation became clearer in my mind. I had speculated even though Gaylan had a large group of supporters, consisting of family and friends, most all of whom were present every day in their fancy high-dollar outfits, one or more of these supporters were actually pulling for us, the prosecution, to prevail.

My reasoning was that I had always believed we recovered most of Preston's money during the warrants, but we never got a big sum of money directly from Gaylan. Logically, somebody in the gallery, someone in Gaylan's inner circle, was thinking, "If Gaylan gets life, I get rich." It would be like hitting the lottery or securing a nice pension.

Oh, well, it was just a theory I was thinking about as I sat there. I was also thinking, wouldn't that be funny if after the verdict of guilty was read, one of Gaylan's "people" lost control and jumped up for joy, because they just got paid.

The jury had received their instructions. They went back to the jury room to deliberate. I thought it would take at least a day, just to go through the evidence, to process it and give everyone in the jury a chance to speak their mind.

If I was on the jury, I would certainly run my deliberations over at least one or two lunch hours because once you go back to the jury room for deliberations, the court orders out lunch for each of the jurors on the government's tab, and I know personally I would not pass up a couple free lunches.

Roscoe and I walked Lilly back to her office, which is in a building adjacent to the federal courthouse. She already had our contact numbers so we could be called to get back to the courthouse for the verdict to be read. Usually, once the jury announces to the judge that a verdict has been reached, a half-hour to forty-five minutes is the delay time in an effort to get the attorneys to call all the people who are of interest in the case back to the courthouse. It is really amazing how many people show up for the reading of the verdict. It truly is standing room only in the court.

It was just before the noon hour, and I decided to go home. Who was going to get upset with that? I had been working fourteen- to sixteen-hour days during the entire trial. I thought they should be happy that I wasn't turning in an overtime slip. I decided to go home and mow my yard for the last time of the year. It was a warm day and I had really neglected my yard during this entire trial and, by nature, I would consider myself a yard guy. I also thought I could pick up my youngest child from school as a surprise.

What a great plan until my phone rang about 4:30. It was Patty, Lilly Lomax's secretary, telling me, "The jury is back. The verdicts will be read in thirty-five minutes."

What I forgot to mention is that I live in a little town about twenty-five minutes away. I quickly calculated the drive time and parking in the downtown area around the courthouse and that I was in my lawn mowing clothes. I thought I would never make it, but I quickly decided that I was going to try, even though I was in jeans and a sweatshirt.

How ironic. The jury had seen Lilly in a different classy outfit every day for the last five weeks, and I had done my best to rotate my suits and sport coats, always giving a professional appearance. I literally broke all traffic laws, pushing it as hard as I could to get to the courthouse. I parked and got through security without a hitch. The guard outside the courtroom told me they were getting ready to read the verdict right now and the judge was on the bench.

I entered the courtroom, walked through the gallery, opened the swinging half-door leading to the defense and prosecution tables and took my seat in front of the jury in my lawn mowing clothes.

The courtroom was filled to the brink. Just as I thought. All the families of the defendants, people from the courthouse, people from law enforcement, and, of course, the media, with all their cameras set up outside the courthouse.

The tension was ten times what it was at the start of trial. There were all sorts of theories on what it meant if the jury came back so quickly. I wasn't much into speculating on those theories, I just wanted to hear it read.

The verdict papers were handed from the foreperson of the jury to the bailiff, who in turn walked the papers to the judge. The judge read the verdict silently and then the papers were turned over to the clerk of the court, who read the verdicts aloud.

It is at this time that I have always enjoyed in my past high-profile trials to turn and watch the defendant or, in this case, the defendants. I turned.

As each count was read, guilty verdicts were announced for Preston Blade and Gaylan Green on all counts of the indictment. Murmurs of objection came from supporters in the gallery. As I watched both Preston and Gaylan, their heads leaned down and their shoulders sank. I think this was the first time they really felt they were defeated.

One verdict was left to be announced: the count against Yessica Tate. And the clerk announced guilty. Yessica's mother could not contain herself and began yelling from the gallery at Preston that it was all his fault.

Once the courtroom had settled down, the option of polling the jurors was given to the defense attorneys, and each juror acknowledged that his or her decision was guilty.

One would think that this was a time to celebrate, but really it was not. It was more relief. So much pressure had been removed. As I knew from the beginning, Lilly Lomax would present the perfect case. Lilly gave interviews to the media outside the courthouse, passing credit on to all those involved in the investigation.

The sentencing would not occur for another six weeks. This would be a key hearing because of the enhancement regarding the murders during the conspiracy, which could boost the sentence to life, if applied. If we did get this life sentence, it may not be necessary to do this entire thing over again in state court for the murders. If they got this life sentence in federal court, the only thing we would gain in state court would potentially be the death penalty, which was no guarantee. We would just have to wait and see how it all played out.

54
PAYING THE PIPER

In the federal court system, the judge does not pronounce a sentence for approximately six to eight weeks. During this time, the pre-trial services office completes a report regarding historical facts on the defendant that can provide both positive and negative information on the convicted person. It is then based on this report and the evidence at trial that the judge assesses the sentence, following guidelines outlined by statute.

Remember that the maximum sentence in our case against Preston and Gaylan was life in prison on three separate counts because of the enhancement Lilly Lomax filed regarding causing the death of another during the course of the conspiracy. These life sentences would be independent of any time received on the narcotics and weapons violations.

All in all, I felt confident that a large number of years would be given to them, but who really knows until the sentence is read.

Yessica Tate was also looking at a total of sixteen years, based on her involvement. I'm sure her attorney was doing his best now to minimize her involvement, trying to make her a victim of Preston. So many people are affected by this negatively: her two children and her mother, who now would have to care for the kids.

As sad as it is, justice must be served. I really did not know how much consideration Yessica would get from the judge, but whatever her sentence was, she had no room to complain because she was given the opportunity to cooperate.

During the weeks of waiting for Preston and Gaylan's sentences, the sentencing of the co-conspirators that testified in court took place. I know in their hearts, they all wanted to get probation, but that was not realistic. They all received varying sentences in federal prison, with the eventual reduction of those sentences for their cooperation. When it was all said and done, the worst sentence was for Rick Ginney, who received eight years, but was reduced to three years because of his cooperation in the investigation.

Sentencing day finally came and, for me personally, so much hung in the balance of this decision. If Preston and

Gaylan received life sentences, then I might be off the hook for another trial on the murder charges in state court.

The three defendants were brought into the courtroom, separately this time, not as a group as they were during trial. The courtroom only had a few family members and media people, nothing like the atmosphere during trial. Security was still tight because there was an opportunity to do something stupid if you are Preston or Gaylan. Each defendant was brought into the courtroom in jail clothes and shackled and cuffed since there was no jury to protect this time. I sure was not planning on ever seeing these people again unless there was a murder trial.

Preston "Shine" Blade was first. The judge quickly acknowledged the attorneys and defendants, then read the sentences on each count. Lilly was writing down totals as the judge was reading. The only thing I heard was three counts of life to run consecutively. When the judge was done, I asked Lilly to explain it, just to confirm what I thought I had heard. Lilly should have brought the adding machine.

When it was all over, Preston was sentenced to three life sentences, plus three hundred years. Preston just stared forward, giving no reaction, as if he was not affected. I knew inside he was feeling real bad.

Gaylan "Nephew" Green was next after a brief recess. I wondered if word would get back to him in his holding cell regarding what had happened to Preston. Gaylan was escorted into the courtroom, looking down the entire time, with no look of optimism about him, so I figured he had gotten the news.

Again, the judge acknowledged all parties and went methodically into sentences on each count, three life sentences plus a lot of years for narcotics and weapons counts. Lilly had to do the math again and Gaylan received three life sentences, plus two hundred fifty years. The difference between his and Preston's sentences was because Preston had a felon status that enhanced his sentence and Gaylan did not.

One more to go, I wondered what Yessica would get. She was escorted into the courtroom also in jail attire, shackles, and cuffs. Her mother was sitting in the front row of the gallery. After the judge acknowledged all parties, Yessica's attorney gave one last oral appeal to the judge regarding motherhood and Yessica's victimization by Preston. The judge politely listened, but I believe she had already made her decision based on the presentence report.

The sentence was read: twelve years in the custody of the Federal Bureau of Prisons. She was remanded to their custody. Yessica began to cry hysterically and asked the judge if she could hug her mother. The Marshals quickly blocked Yessica's mother, who stood up to reach out to her daughter. Yessica was swiftly taken away.

It was all over, except for appeals, which would go on for years. I wasn't too worried about them. The case was too solid, the prosecution was solid, and our case would stand up to any tests down the road.

There were only two more issues that I could think of as the sentencings ended. Should we have the murder trial in state court, where the only thing to gain would be the death penalty? It was decided to drop the state murder case. It was the most logical call by Georgeann Goldstein for several reasons. First, it probably saved the taxpayers a quarter-million dollars to not have that trial. Second, the likelihood of getting the death penalty was small, which would just leave more life sentences. And third, it saved all the work and effort it would take to recreate the same trial again. Plus, as time passes, witnesses disappear, memories fade, and the case just may never be that good again.

The last thing I'm waiting for is the phone call. I don't know when it will come. Maybe in one year, maybe in two years, maybe longer. I don't know when, but I do know it will come. You do not piss off a Mexican cartel, killing their people and stealing millions of dollars and dope from them. Somebody will get their revenge and kill Gaylan and Preston in federal prison.

Right after the murders, they wanted revenge, but could not figure out who to go after in Omaha. Well, that's all changed now. Preston "Shine" Blade and Gaylan "Nephew" Green were not only identified for them, but with a quick search of the Federal Bureau of Prisons website, an inmate location can be obtained. That's all they need to order the payback. It is just a matter of time.

EPILOGUE

This massive case was over and justice had been served. That was enough for me. Little did Roscoe and I know, but N.S. Boss submitted our names and the investigation to be considered for some commendations. Roscoe and I were awarded two honors.

First, we were representing the State of Nebraska at the National TOP COPS Awards given by the National Association of Police Organizations (hosted by John Walsh of *America's Most Wanted*) and received a TOP COPS Honorable Mention in Washington, D.C., for work on this case. This was definitely fine with us because as each investigation was summarized at the award ceremony, it seemed as if all the other winners had been shot in the line of duty.

Our second award came from the Department of Justice—the L.E.C.C. Award for Advancing Justice and Cooperation in Nebraska Law Enforcement. Both awards were very humbling and graciously received.

Roscoe (left) and I receive the L.E.C.C. Award for Advancing Justice and Cooperation in Nebraska Law Enforcement for this case.

But the most rewarding praise came about a year after the trial. My teenage daughter, who played competitive softball, was starting her winter practices. So, as the families gather around the perimeter of the practice facility, the parents from the previous year are greeting each other after the off season. There are usually one or two new families joining the team, so this is where you first meet them.

I felt one of the new fathers looking at me, but I just kind of brushed off that feeling. As soon as I stood closer to the guy, he said, "I know you." Not the words an old undercover cop wants to hear. I quickly looked at his face, trying to process if this was some old collar I had and was it gonna get ugly right there. He can see I'm trying to figure out who he is, but I just couldn't.

He then said, "You don't remember me."

I responded, "No. Did I arrest you?"

He laughed and then said, "I was on the jury for the triple murder."

I was so relieved. No conflicts. This father then says to me, "That was an amazing case. You did a hell of a job." That was the greatest reward. Just those words, "You did a hell of a job." Justice was indeed served.

Gaylan Green is serving his three life sentences, some two hundred plus years, at a federal prison with the highest-rated level of security in the Federal Bureau of Prisons where the inmates have closed control movement. Preston Blade is also serving three life sentences plus some two hundred years in a separate high-level-security federal prison.

Yessica Tate is serving out her sentence in a low-security federal prison.

Some of the other defendants have served their time and are now back on the street.

And the three victims? Primitive wooden-cross markers mysteriously appeared at the wooded site where the three burning bodies were discovered. Cars speed by every day, up the roller-coaster hills and down, the drivers never realizing that the biggest drug case in Omaha's history started (and ended) with the discovery of a "brush fire" just to the side of the road.

Today, cars speed by the site where three bodies
were found burning.

The brush is denser now, the trees more protective of the horror that took place on this ground. Yellow plastic lilies, once part of a graveside-like bouquet, are trampled in the undergrowth. And a simple white stone engraved with a figure of Jesus lies to the side of one of the wooden crosses.

Today, this is the remote spot
where police found three bodies burning.

The barber shop still sits unoccupied in the strip mall next to the yellow house with garish blue shutters, where a young family now lives. The driveway is still filled with ruts and holes, the carport roof long gone. And the worn path through the hedge from the carport to the barber shop has grown back full and dense.

The homicide crew completely split up soon after the trial. Roscoe had been transferred to the narcotics unit, and Padre Thorton and Sgt. Bogowski retired. Isadore Demann was promoted to sergeant and assigned to run a cold case squad, where he was very smart to recruit Scrap Iron to his crew.

The vacant barber shop. The roof of the yellow house can be seen above the dense hedges. A path through the hedge between the two has grown over. The stoop where various players described sitting is the short brick wall.

Brandon Sweet also retired after spending some eighteen years in narcotics. Jimmy Quinn worked in narcotics for three years after the trial and his desk sat right next to Roscoe's until he retired. N.S. Boss, after his promotion to captain, soon became Chief of Police. Lilly Lomax is still prosecuting and kicking butt. Georgeanne Goldstein earned a District Court Judgeship.

The yellow house.

I worked one more big case, writing a wiretap on a rival gang of the 40th Avenue Crips. The case federally indicted over thirty dough heads. I decided after that case, the timing was right and I retired too.

I certainly don't miss the bureaucratic bullshit at the department, but I sure do miss being a detective.

My narcotics crew (left to right): Jimmy Quinn, me, Tommy Stash, and Brandon Sweet.

ACKNOWLEDGMENTS

Acknowledgments have proven to be a very difficult closing to this project for me. Not because I don't want to thank all those who have helped me along the way, not only with this book, but in my life. So I first and foremost must put out a disclaimer apologizing if I forget anyone. I plan to keep this brief.

Thanks to all the law enforcement officers I've worked with both with the Omaha Police and other agencies. To those who have gone the extra mile, given 110 percent, serving the public and promoting justice, it has been my honor to work with you.

To support services staff, thank you for making me look better than I probably was. These groups include property/evidence, the Eastern Nebraska Forensic Lab, the University of Nebraska Medical Center's Human DNA Identification Laboratory, the U.S. Attorney's Office Technical Services, and all the typists. Thank you, Sheri White, first a good friend and second a great typist. You made my book drafts look great.

The highly skilled Omaha Police Crime Lab technicians who worked on this case were Daniel Bredow, James Brady, Laura South-Casey, and Stephen Vaccaro.

Sincere thanks to all the prosecutors I've been privileged to work with in my career. I've seen many personalities and styles. Some I even clashed with. I learned from you all.

Maria Moran and Leigh Ann Retelsdorf, my go-to prosecutors. Always telling me just the way it was: "I need more evidence." But always with a smile. You both are at the top of your professions. I always loved watching you guys do your thing in court. Expertise, style, presence, attitude when needed. The bad guy didn't stand a chance. Thank you for all your help over the years.

Thanks to my guy at the FBI, Special Agent Dick Heideman. Your creative writing skills always kept the money coming so the investigative process never stopped. You're old school and definitely one of the good ones.

Now specifically a few coworkers and bosses—we definitely fought the good fight together: James Quaites, Mark Lang, Mark Langan, Ken Kanger, Todd Kozelichki, Steven Henthorn, William Jadlowski, and Alexis Hayes.

My homicide crew (left to right) at the entrance to Bedrock:
me, Padre Thornton, Chief of Police N.S. Boss, Scrap Iron Golic,
Roscoe Hogan, Isadore Demann, and Sgt. Harry Bogowski.

I would never forgive myself if I didn't mention my first two partners walking the beat in Logan Fontenelle Projects. We were straight out of the academy. It's crazy how our lives have gone in different directions, but as soon as we get together, that brotherly bond takes over. Thank you for being my partners: Jeff Saalfeld and Adam Kyle—call sign Beat Patrol 10.

Robert Laney, a good cop but more important a good man. A partner who always had my back and wasn't afraid to work hard, long hours. Your memory is like glue. You were always able to clearly reference some past event. What an asset. You will always be like a brother.

Thanks to Shawn Fisher, in the Crime Analysis Unit, for producing all my graphs and charts and making me look smarter than I am.

To my parents, I don't know the words to say what I feel. You provided me so much support and love that has been the foundation to make my life good. Always know you did a great job with your kids, and sorry, mom, about all the swear words in the book.

I pin a Sergeant's badge on my wife at her promotion—one of my proudest moments on the job.

To my four children, you are my pride and joy. I apologize for all the things I missed when you were small because of the job. As I watch you all grow, you make a parent feel such inner peace. I have seen so many negatives in my career that seeing how you have developed into good productive people is a great feeling for a parent. But remember, always be humble and treat others with respect. I never want to miss a teaching moment. Love you.

Last but first in my heart, my wife. I know I have been a challenge at times when my obsession with the job got out of hand. You are the most genuine person I know. A quality so rare in life. A perfect wife, mother, and cop. I love you and thanks for all you do. I will make good on Hawaii!

ABOUT THE AUTHOR

Author Brian Bogdanoff retired from the Omaha Police Department after over twenty years of service. He holds a bachelor's degree in criminal justice from the University of Nebraska at Omaha and graduated from the Omaha Police Academy. Before his service as a homicide detective, Bogdanoff was an undercover narcotics detective for the City of Omaha.

Bogdanoff's police work has been awarded many times by the Law Enforcement Coordinating Committee, a group dedicated to "enhancing the overall effectiveness of the criminal justice system." He also received a TOP COPS Honorable Mention in 2007 for his work on this case from the National Association of Police Organizations.